SCUFFLE - BOOKS

Mushroom Houses

A Coloring Book for Artist who love to color.

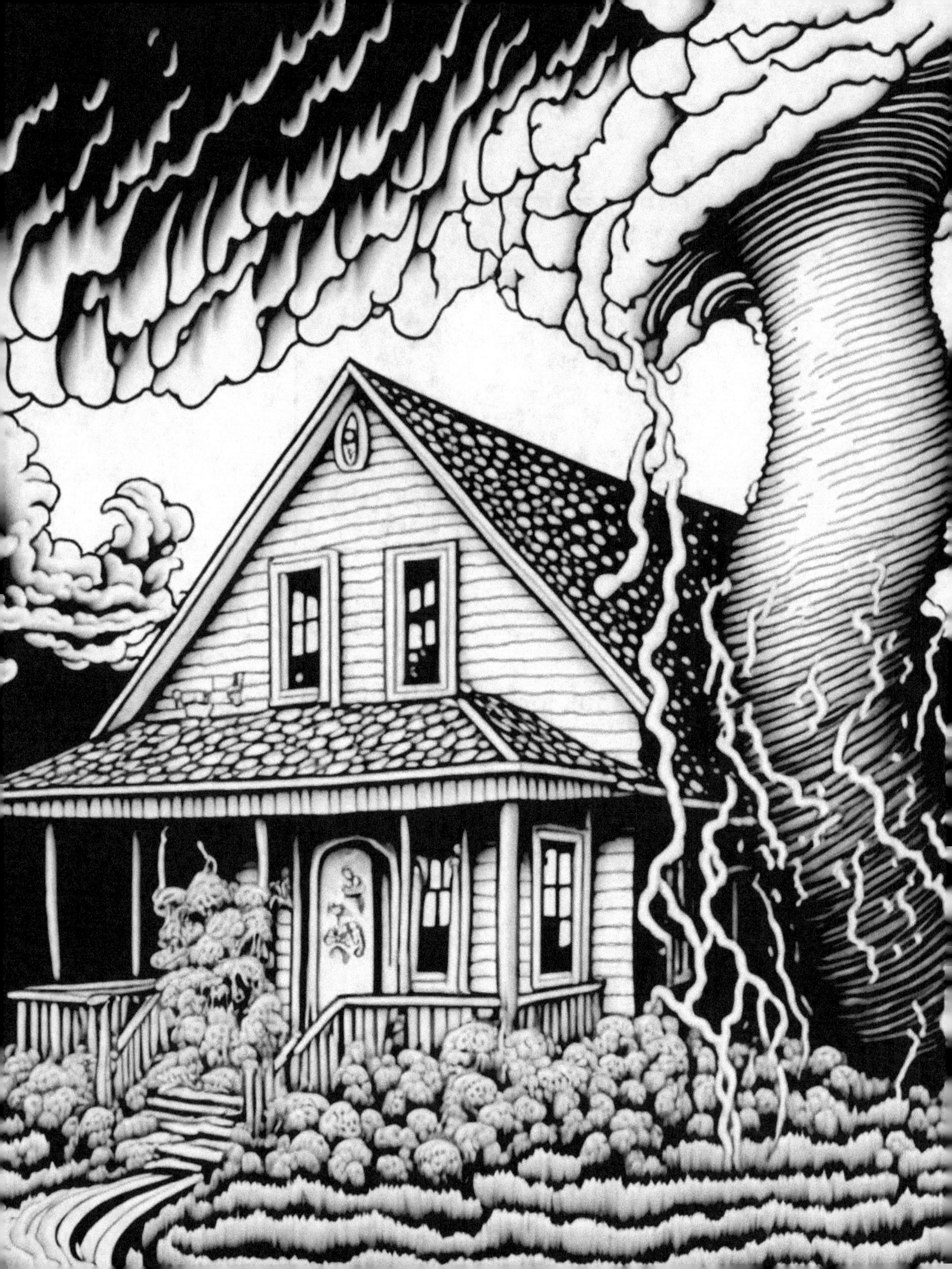

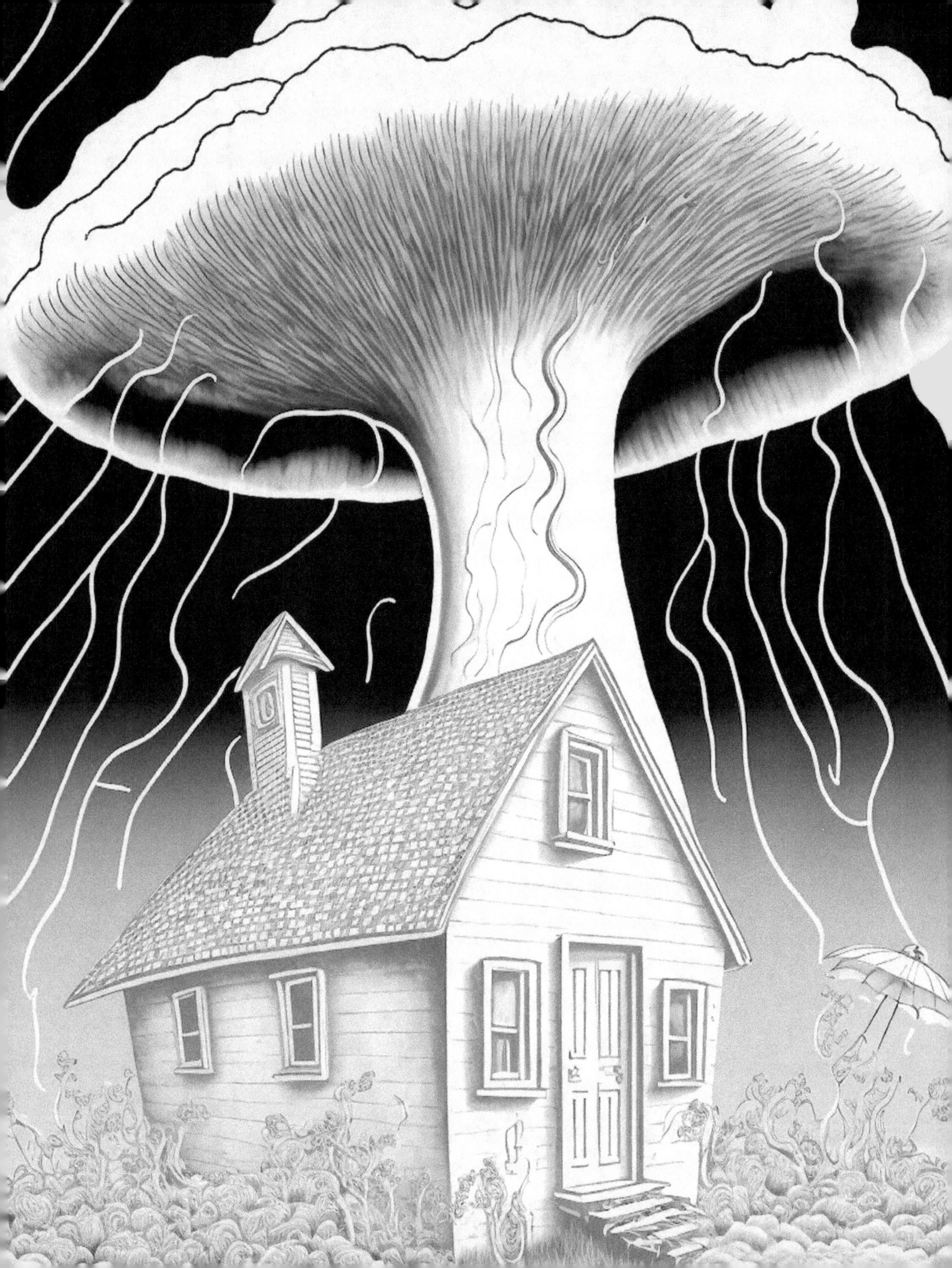

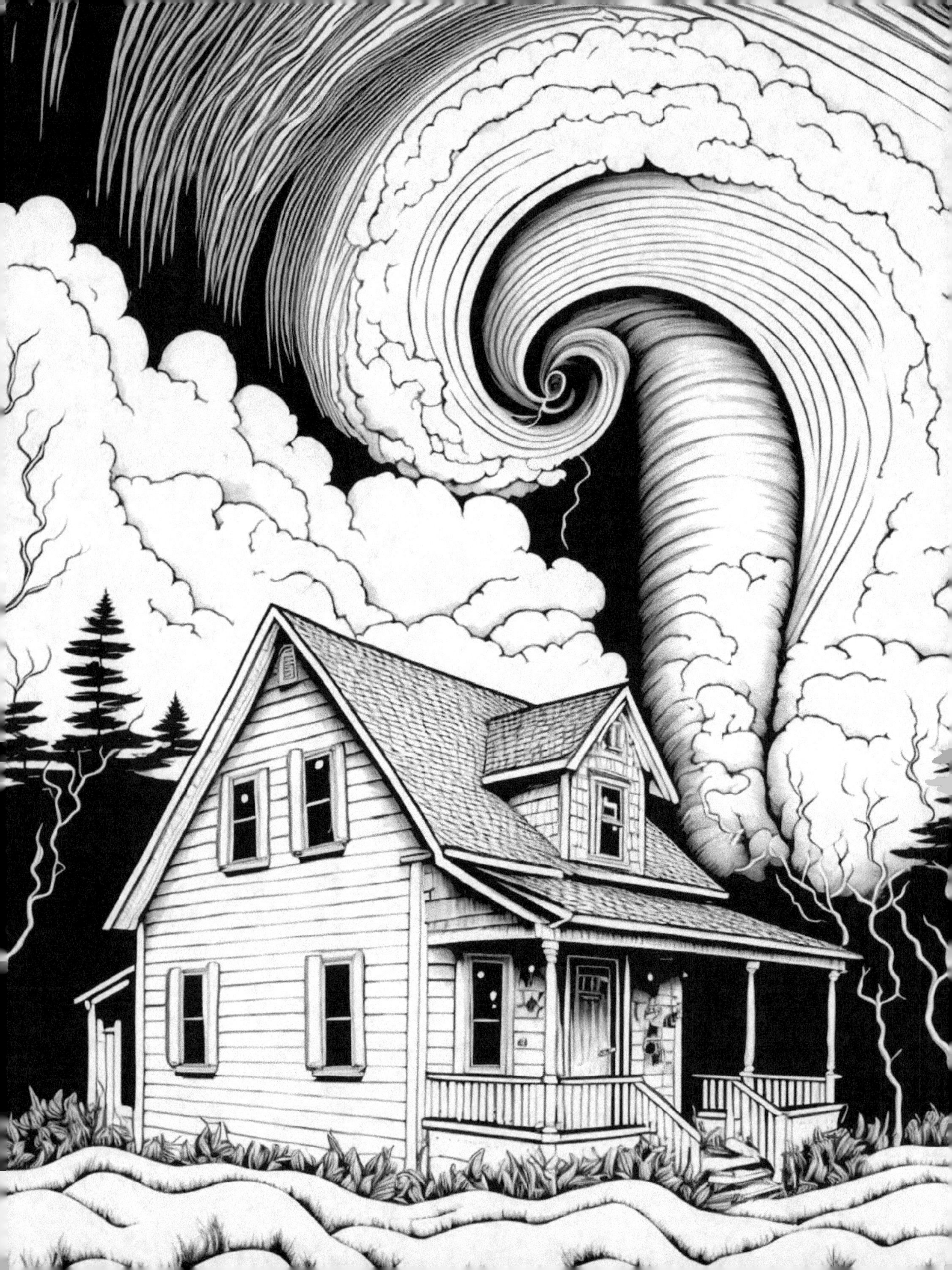

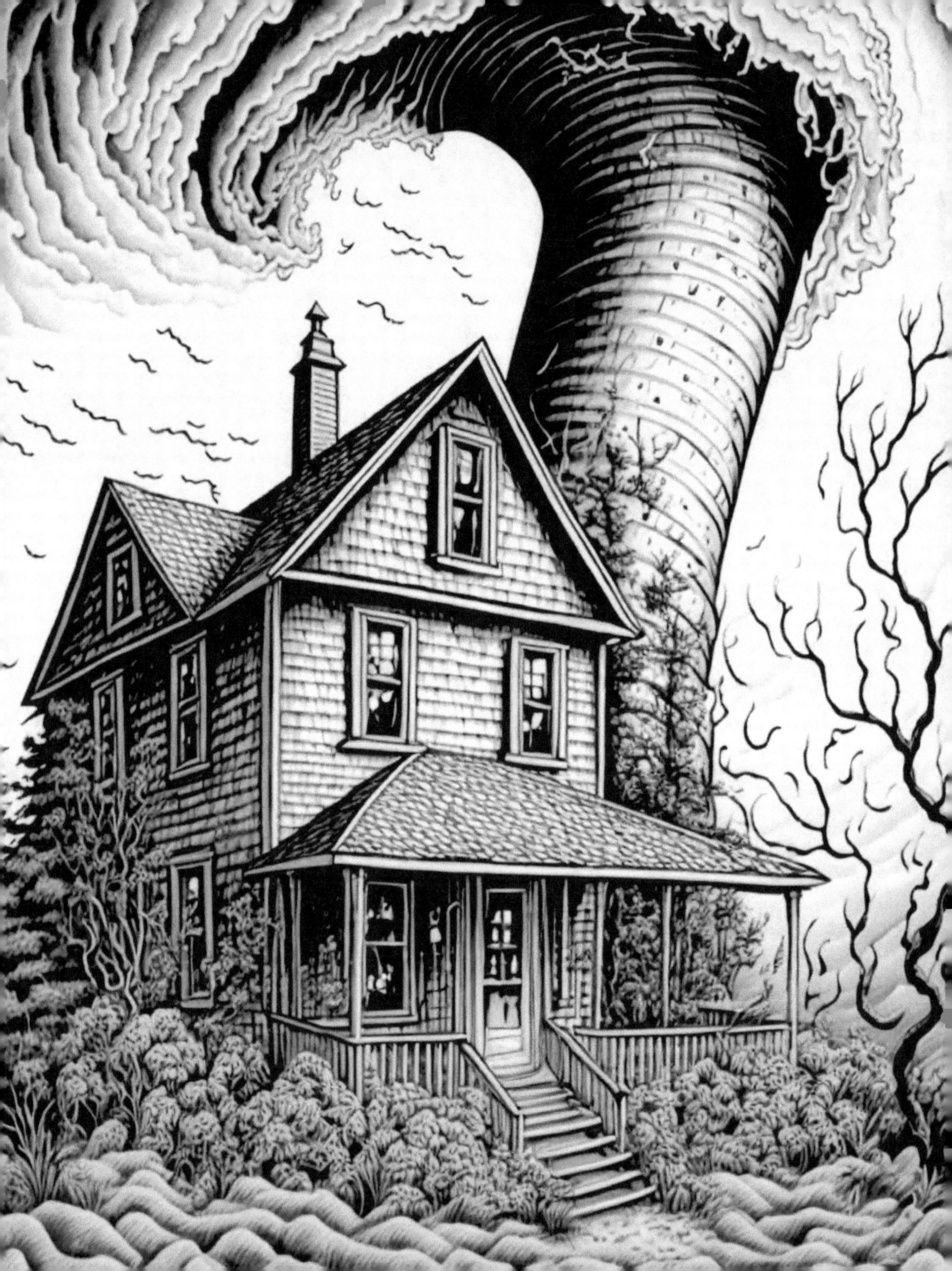

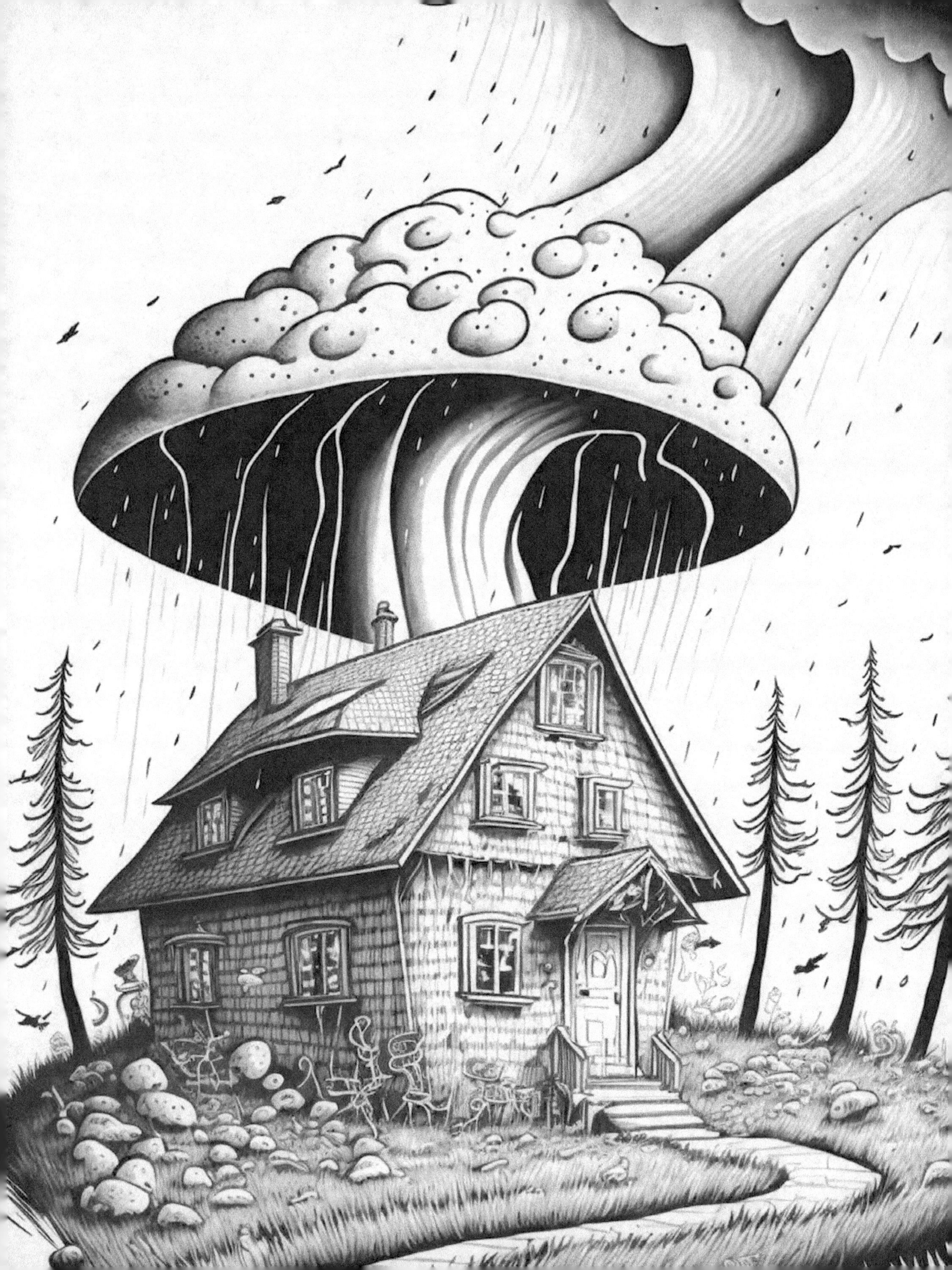

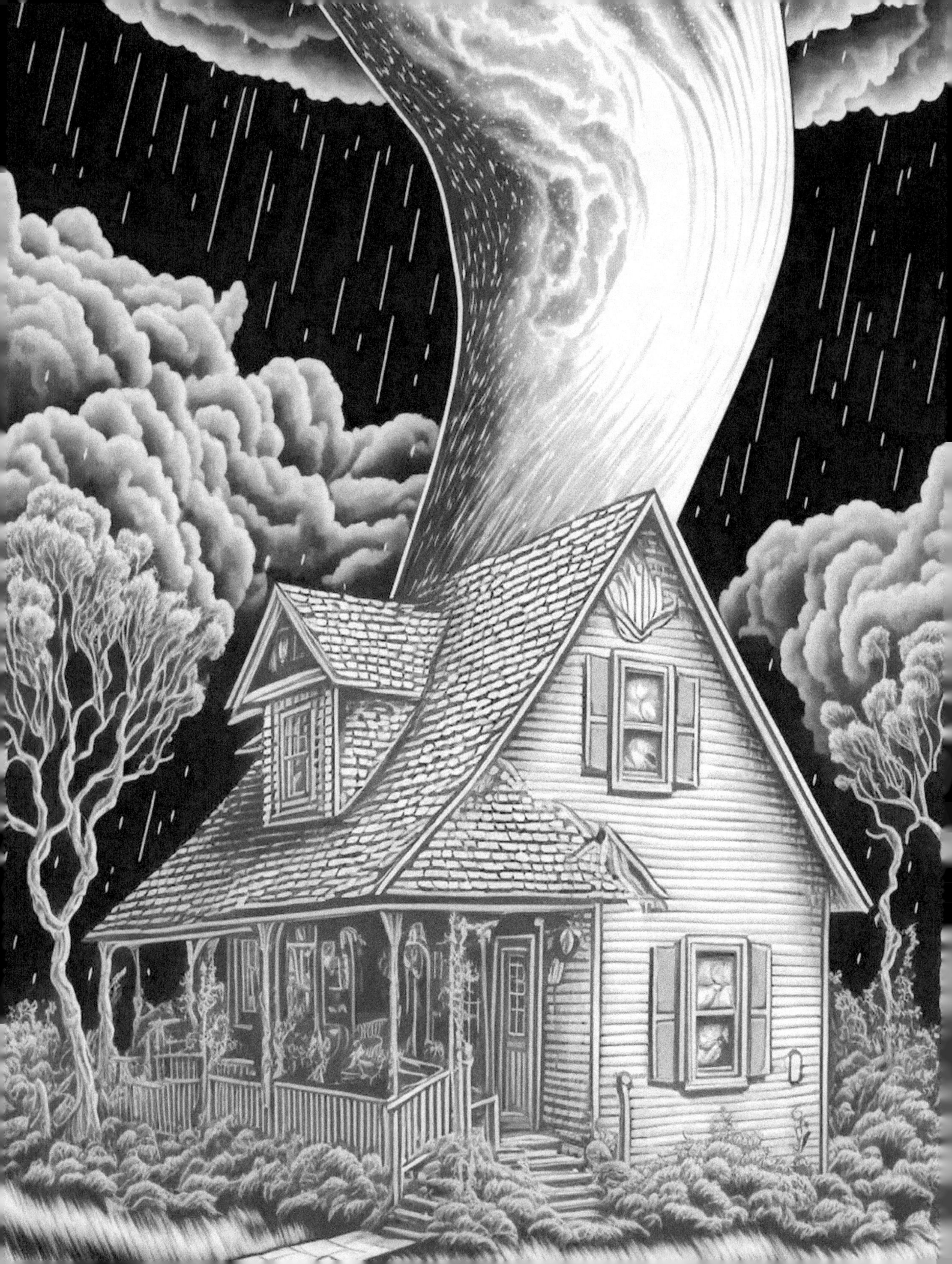

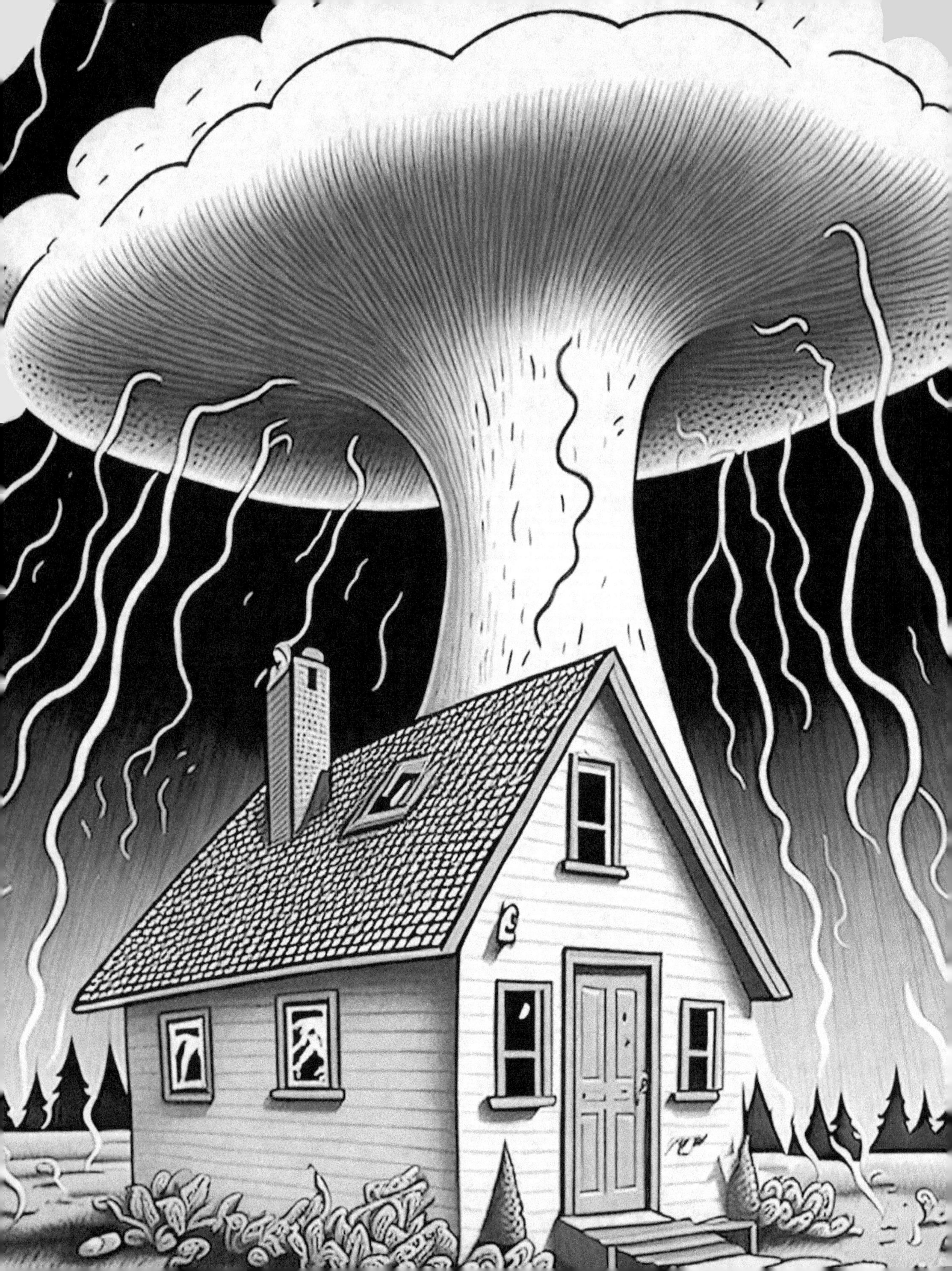

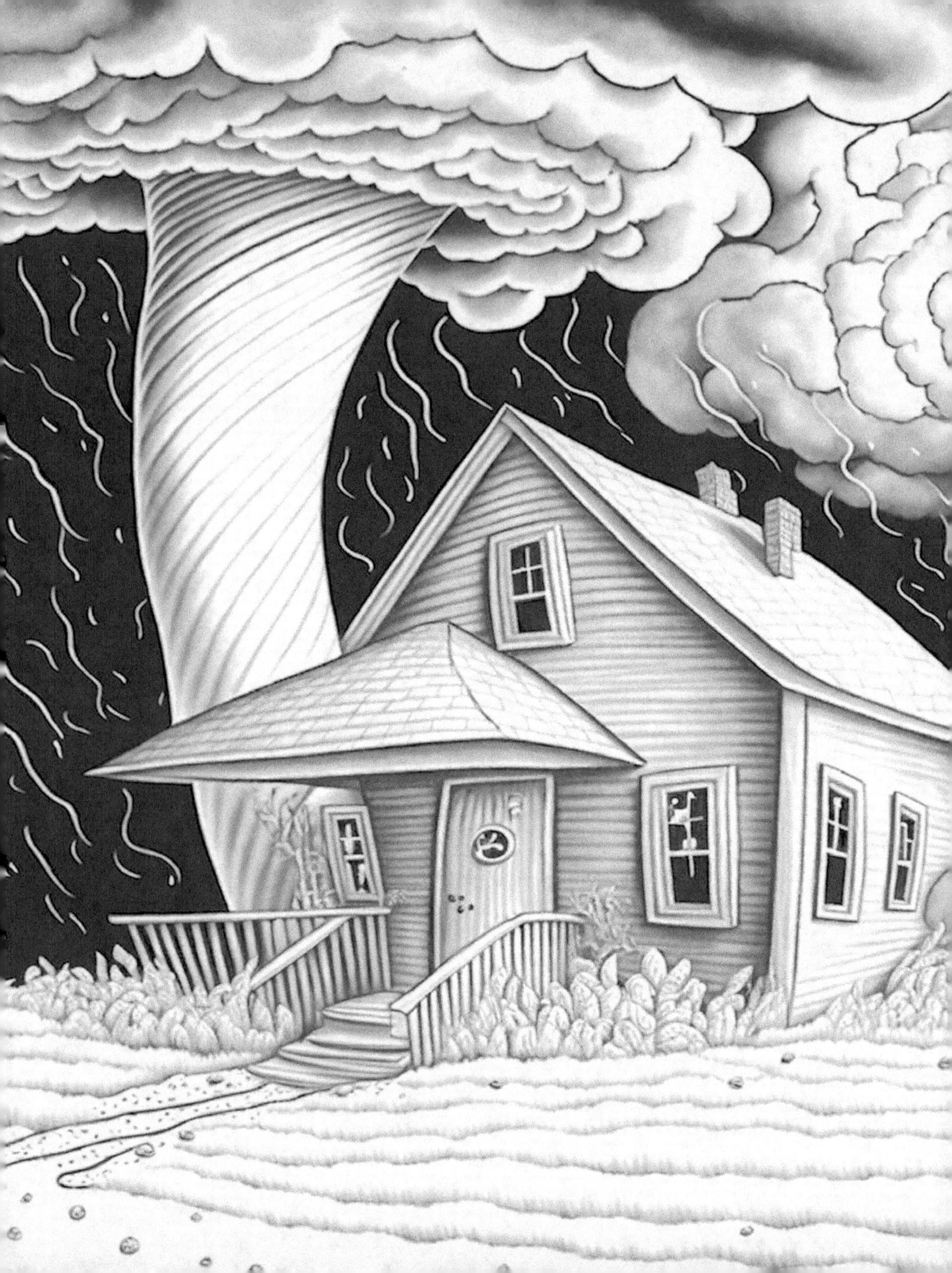

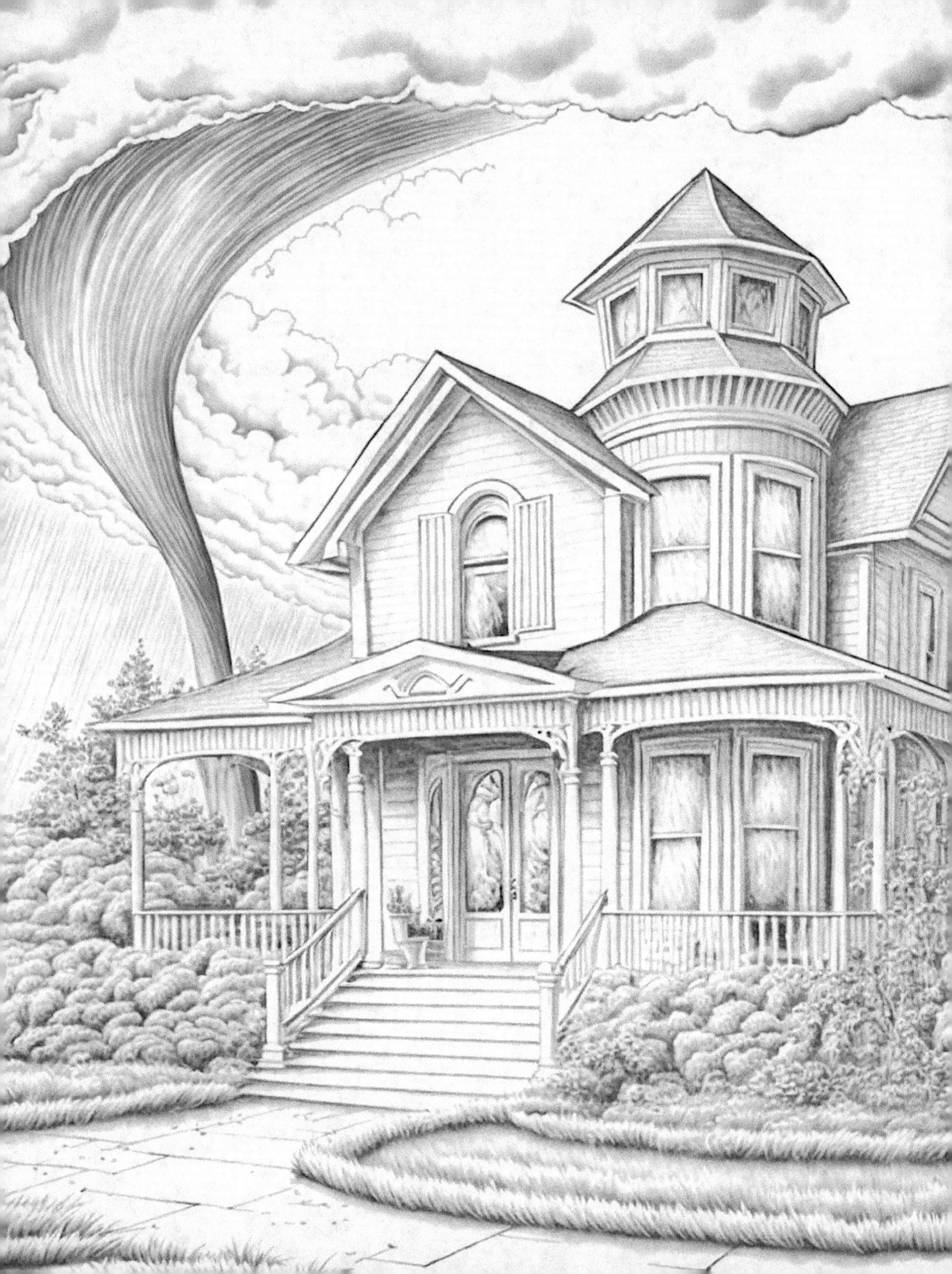

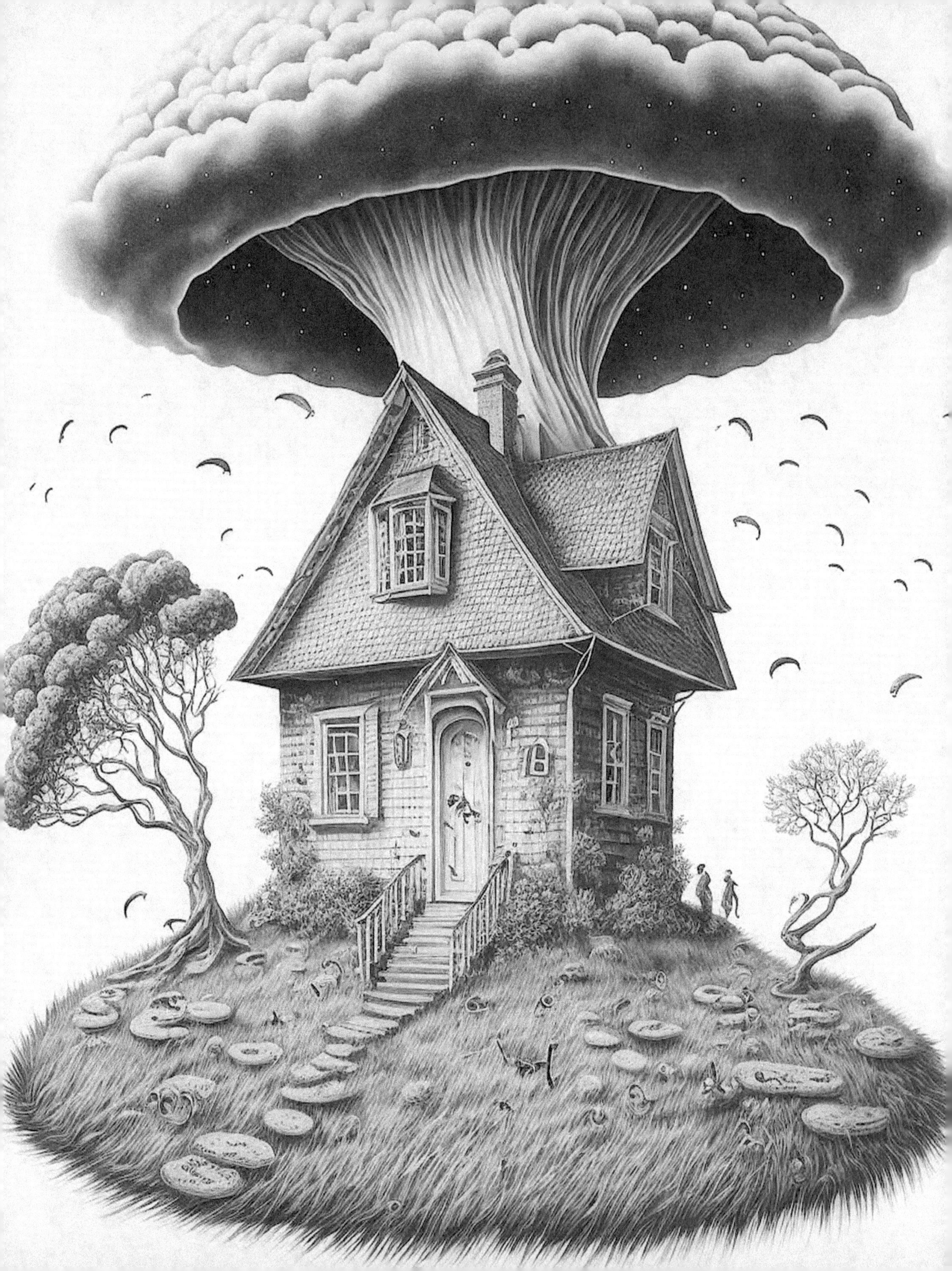

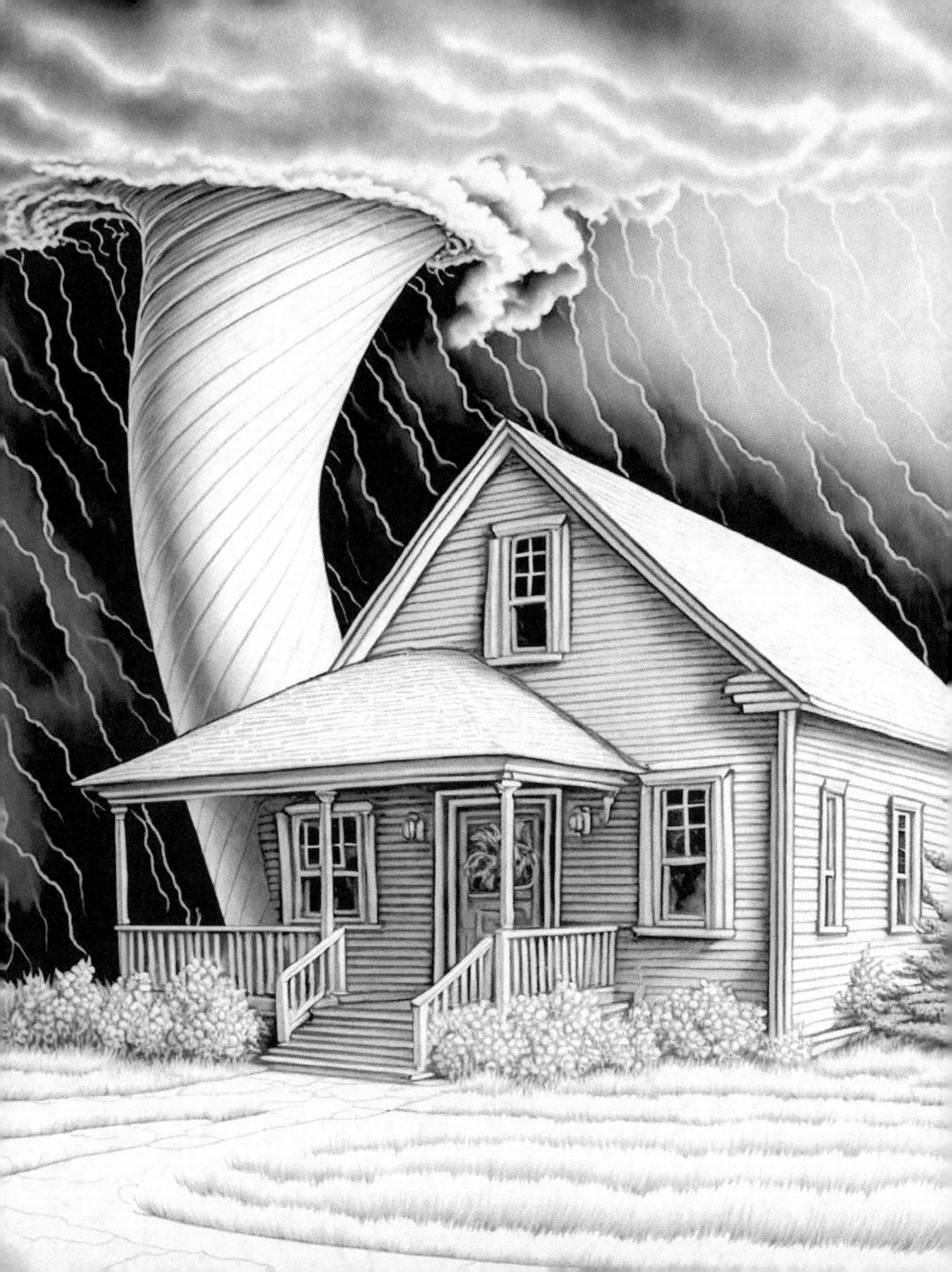

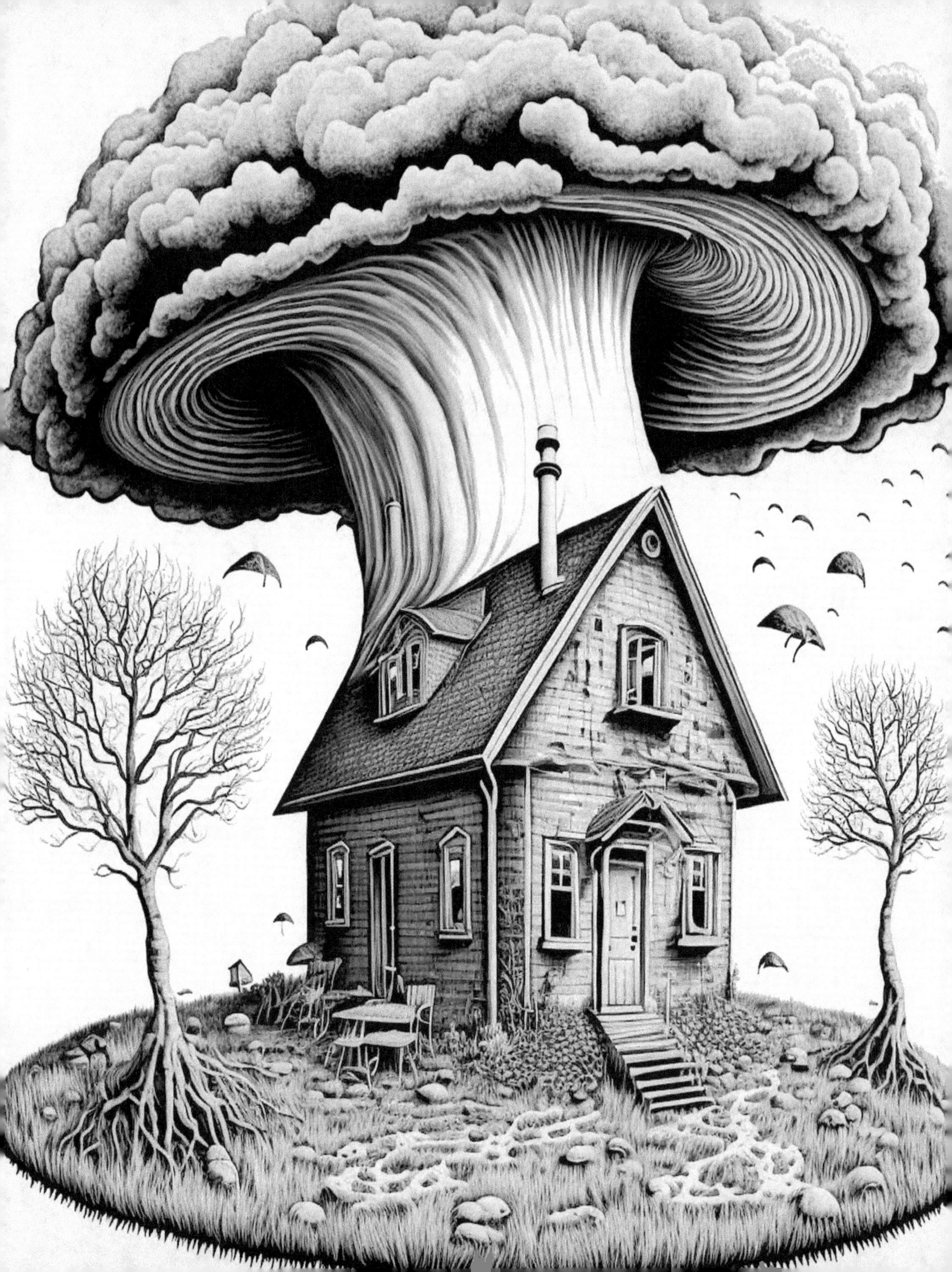

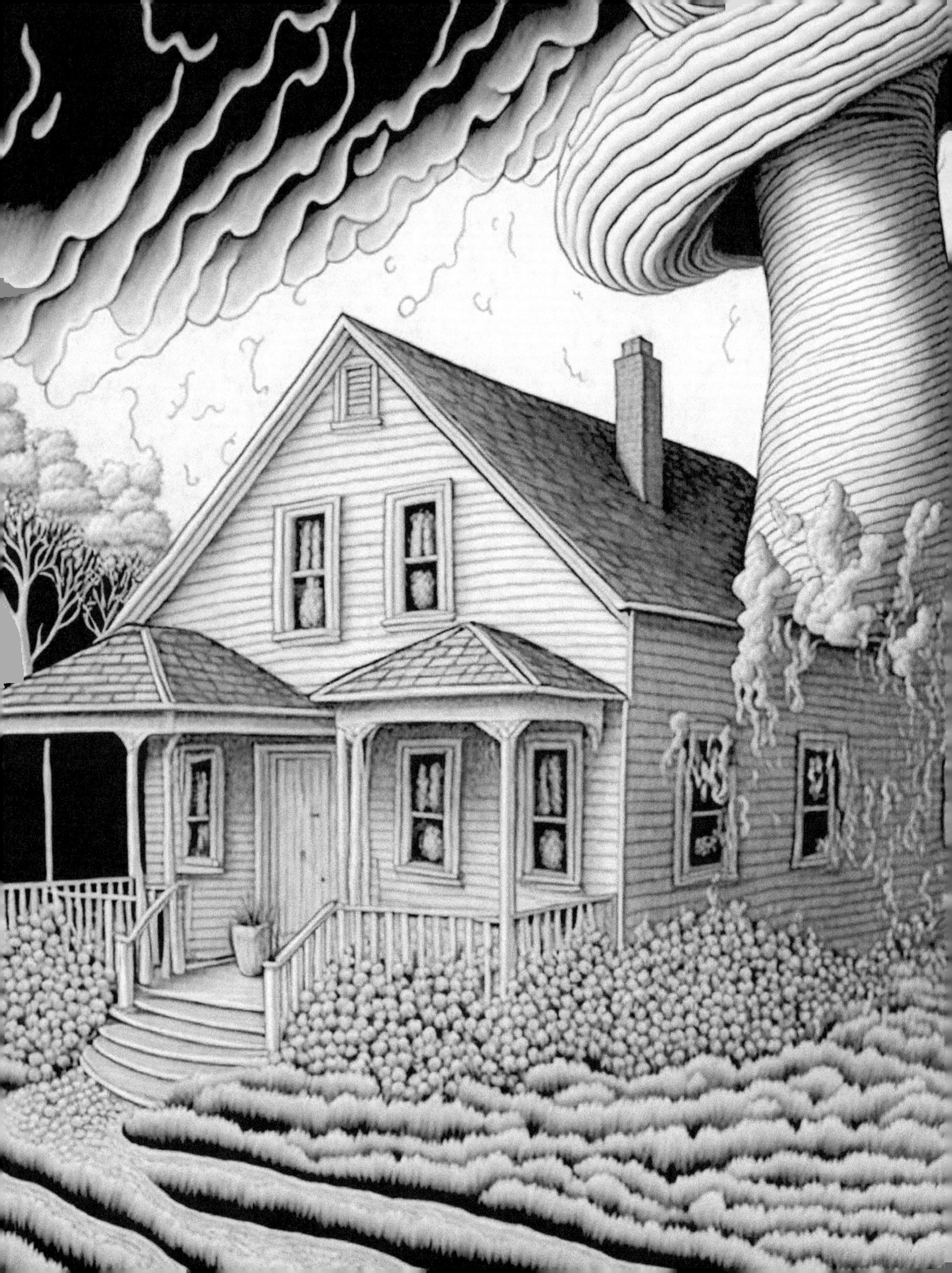

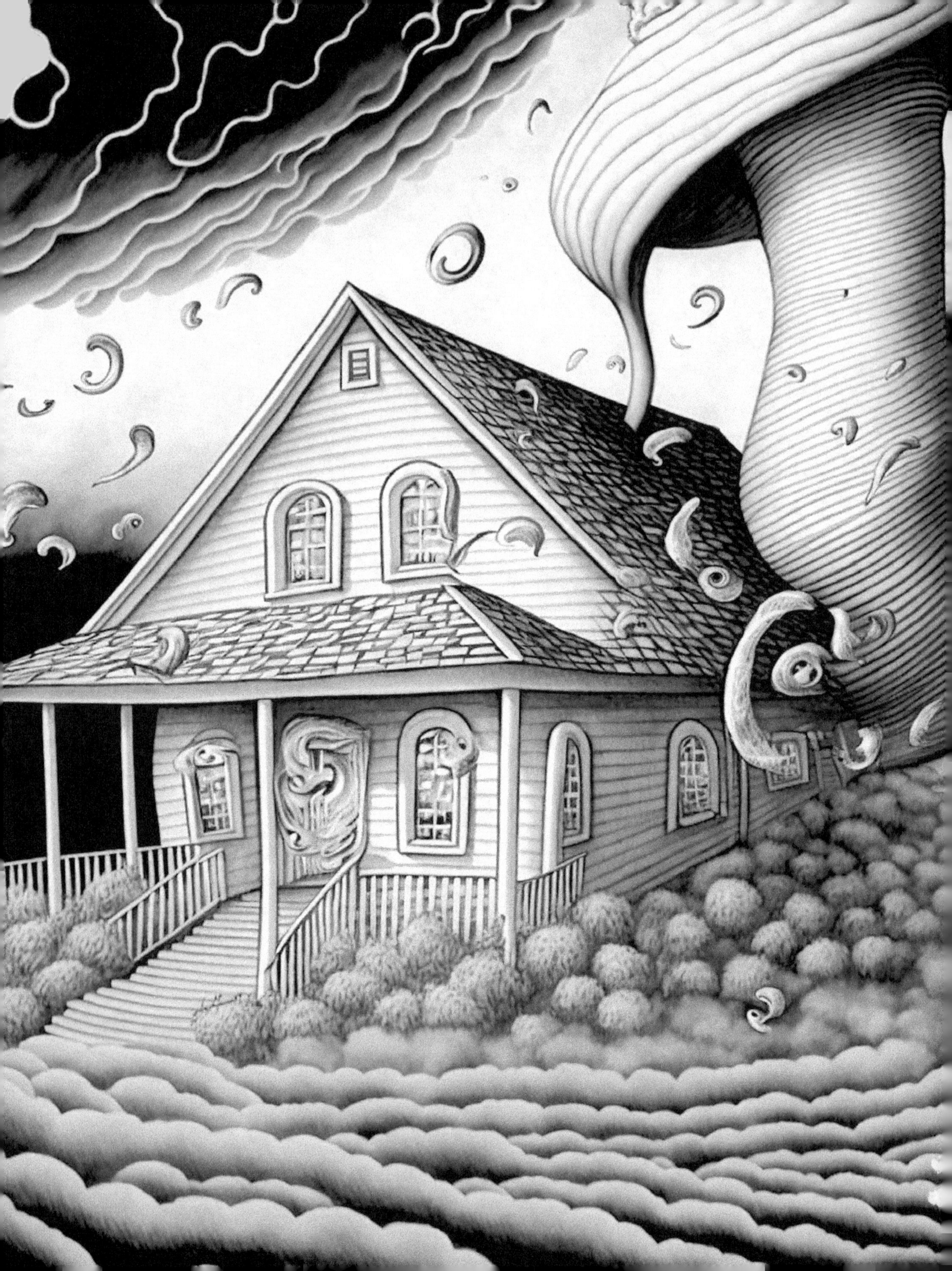

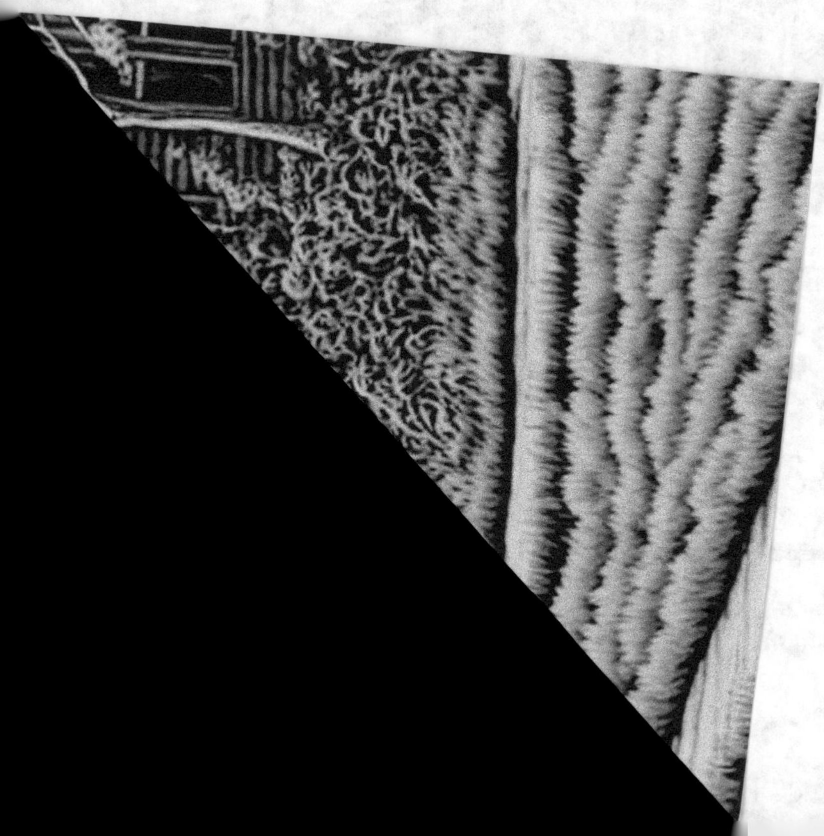

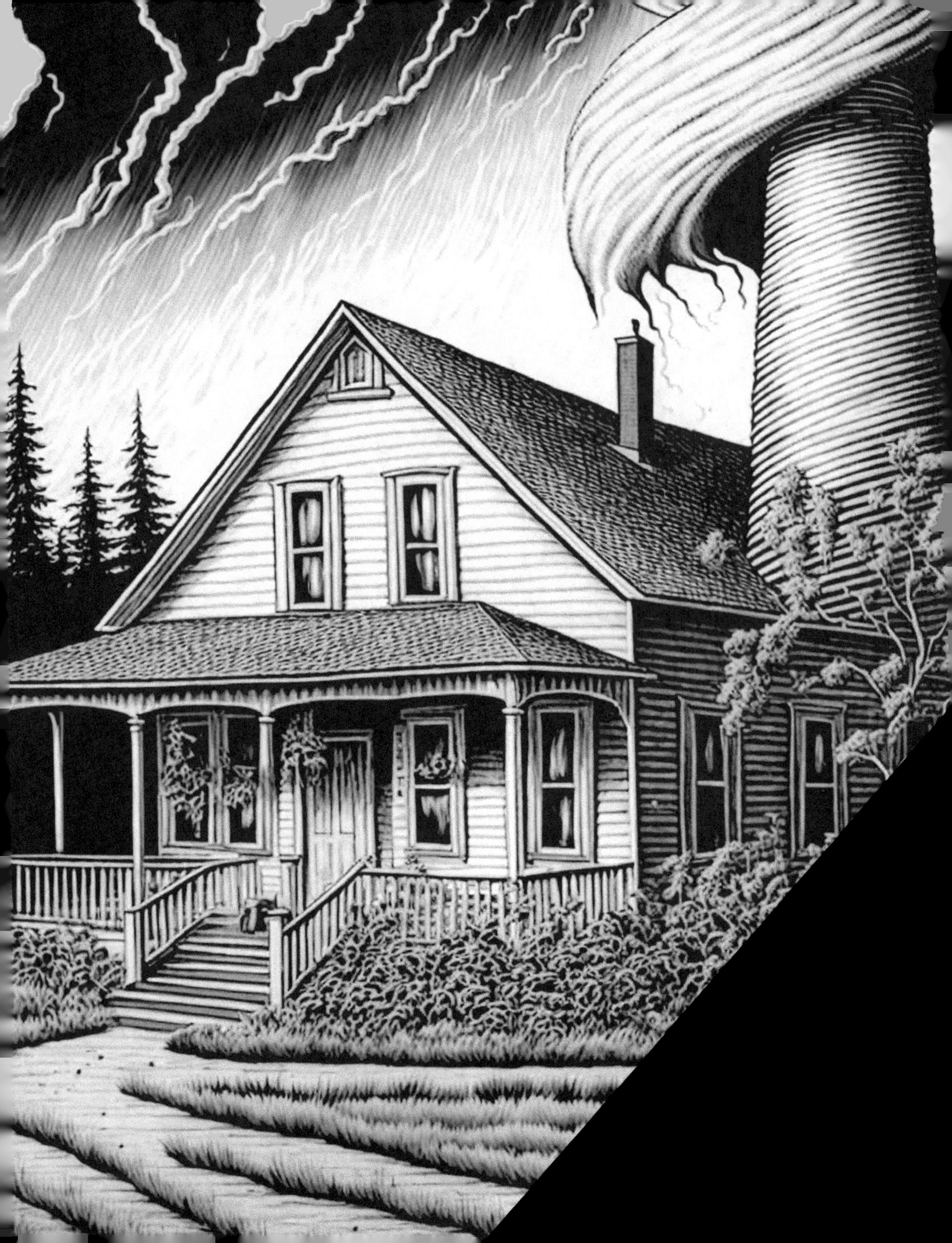

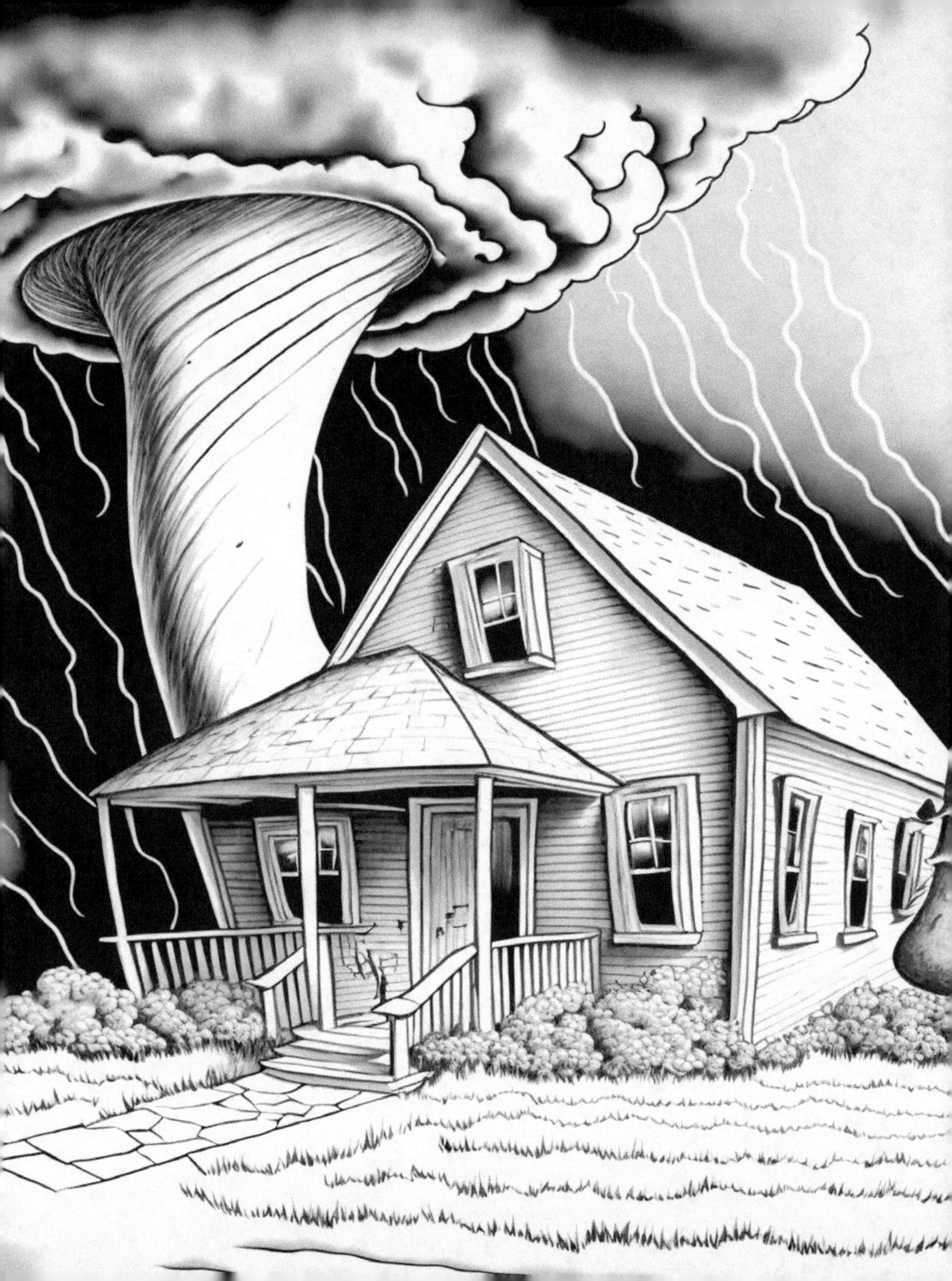

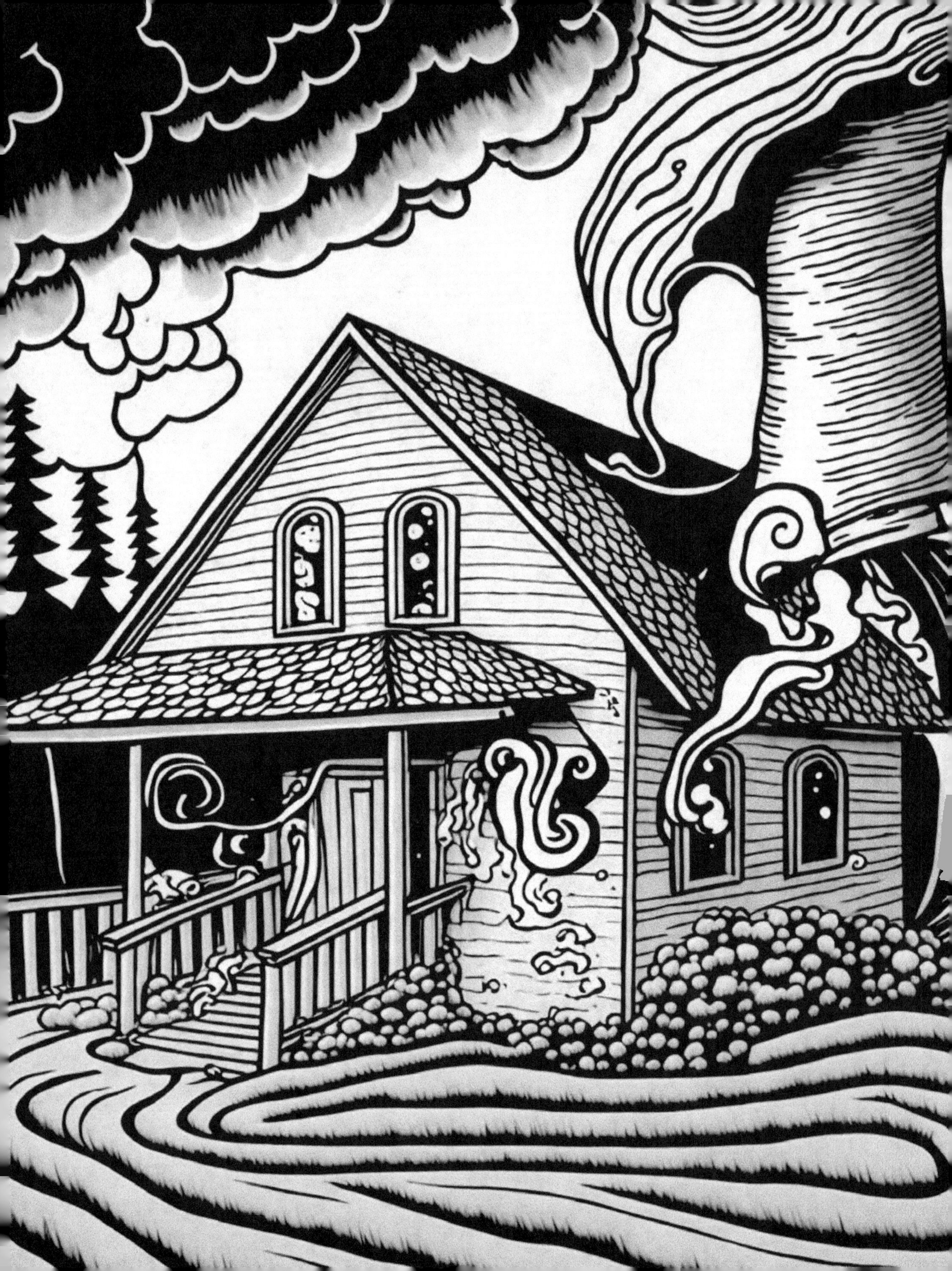

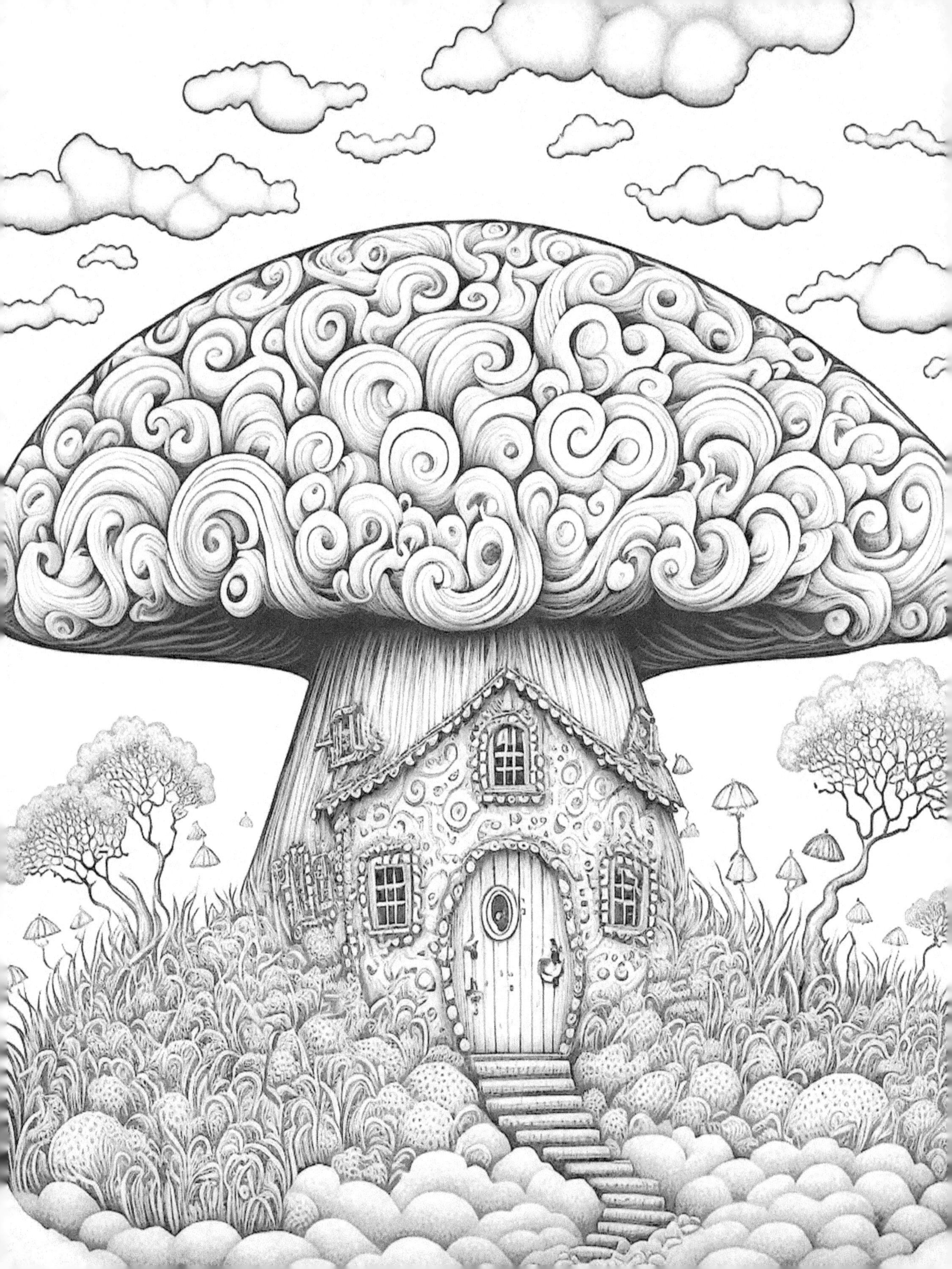

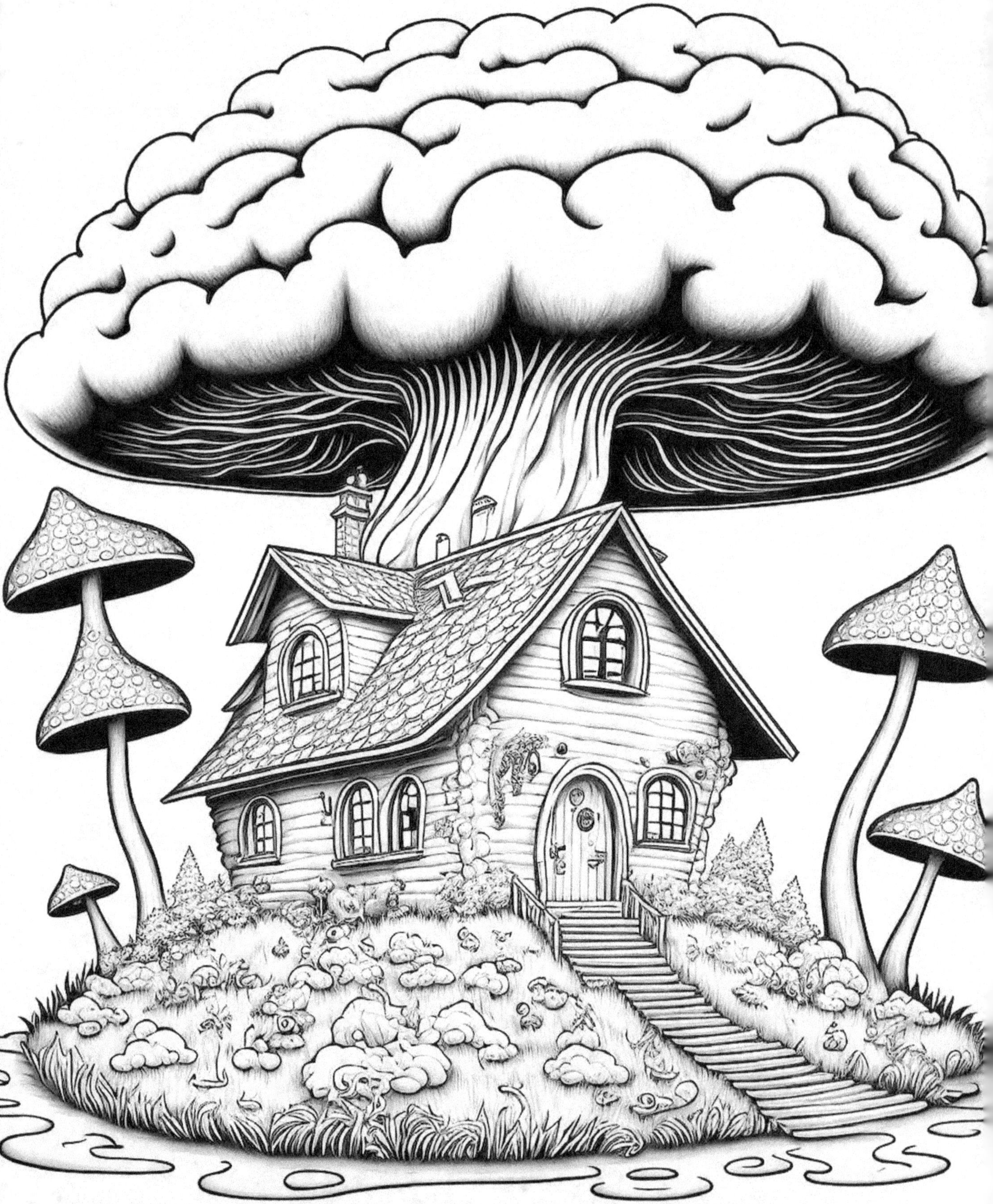

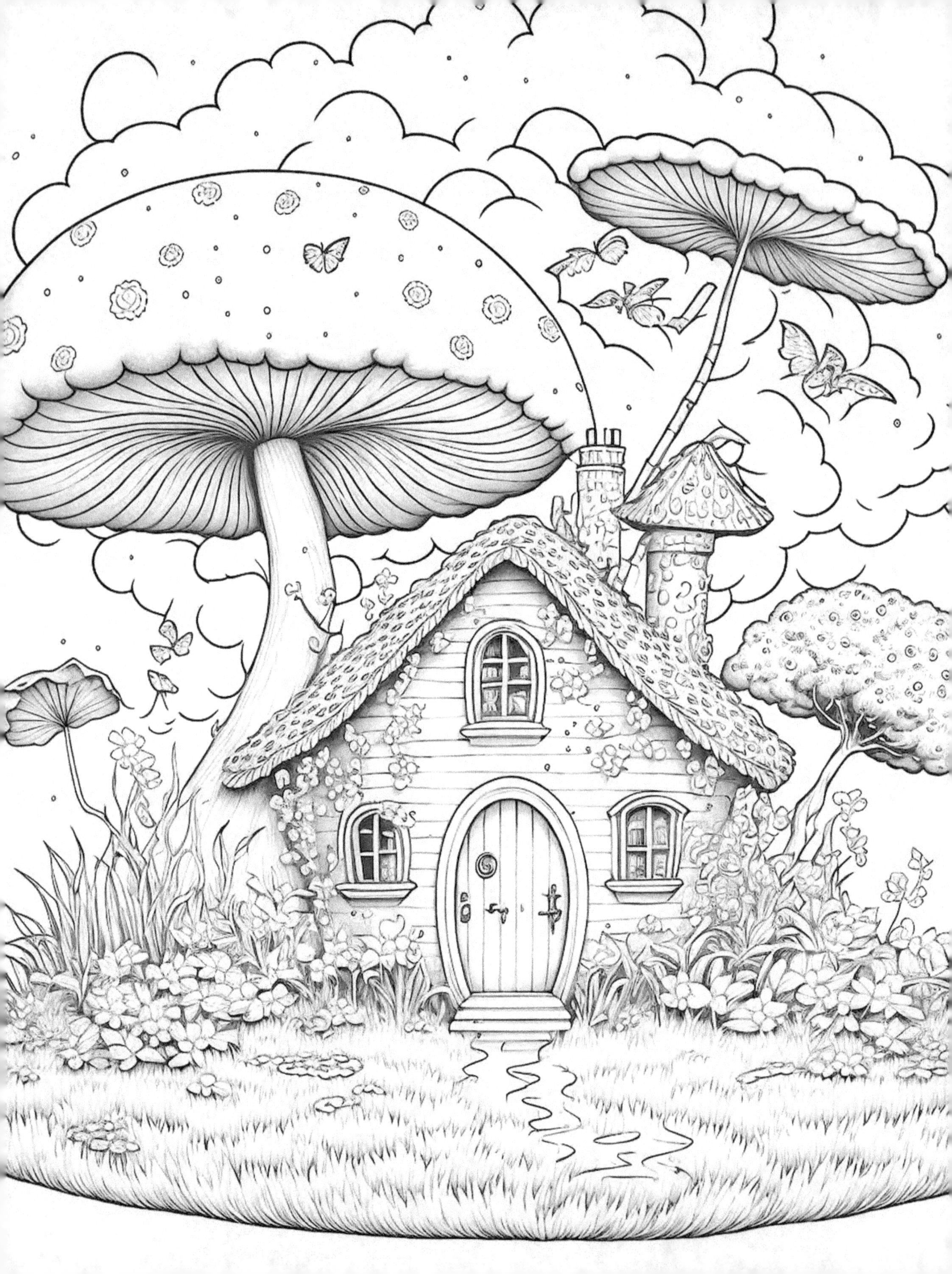

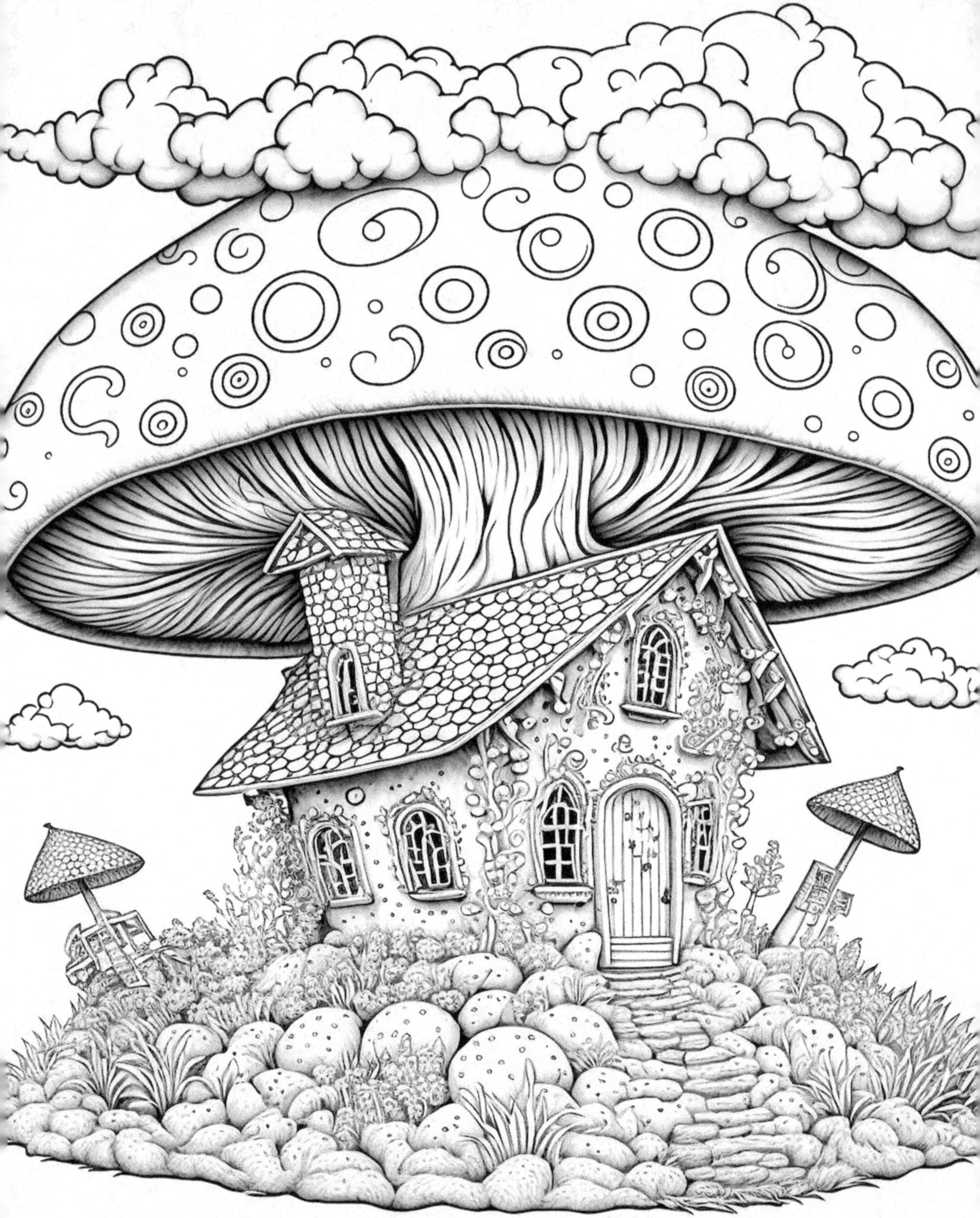

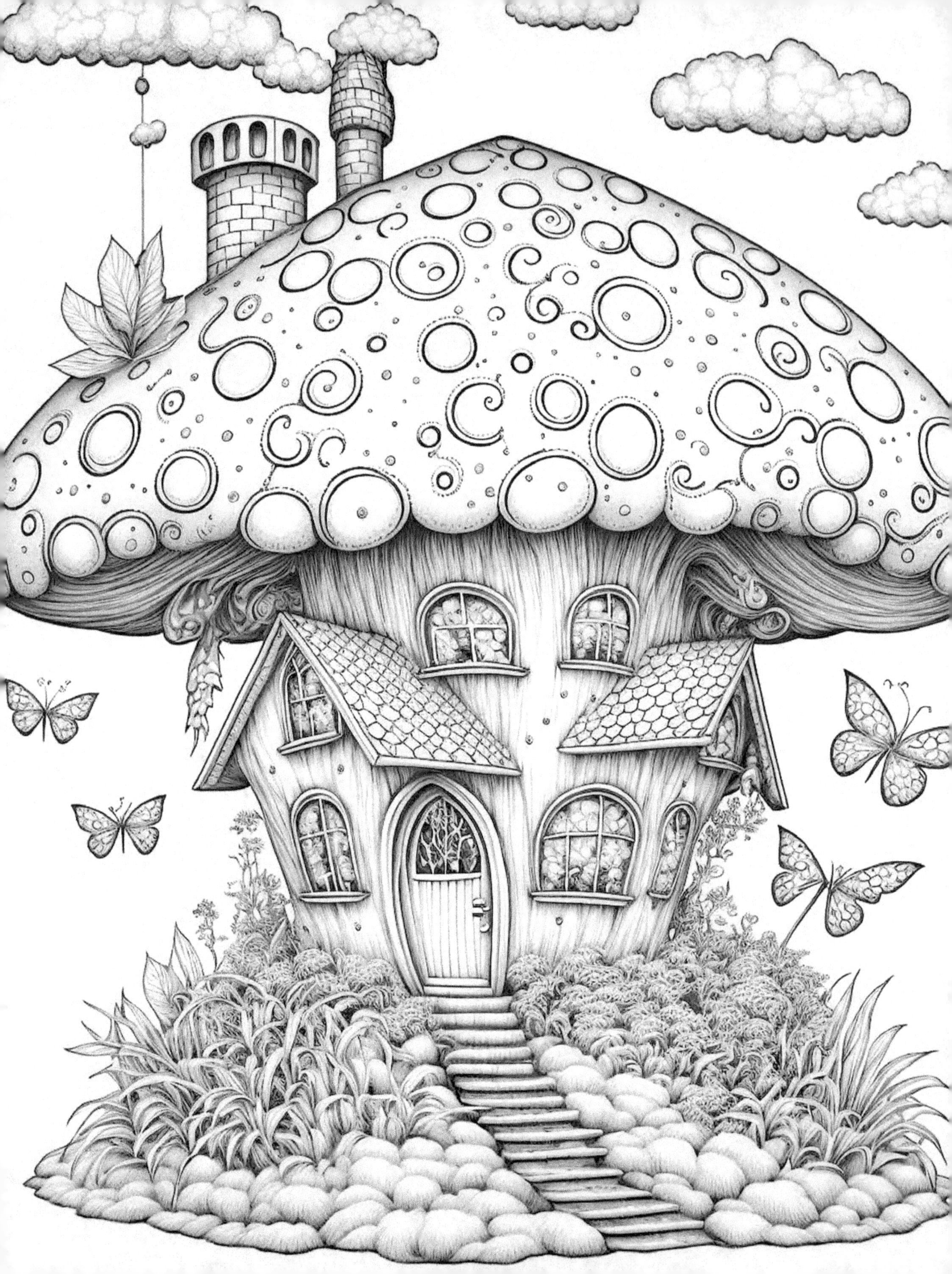

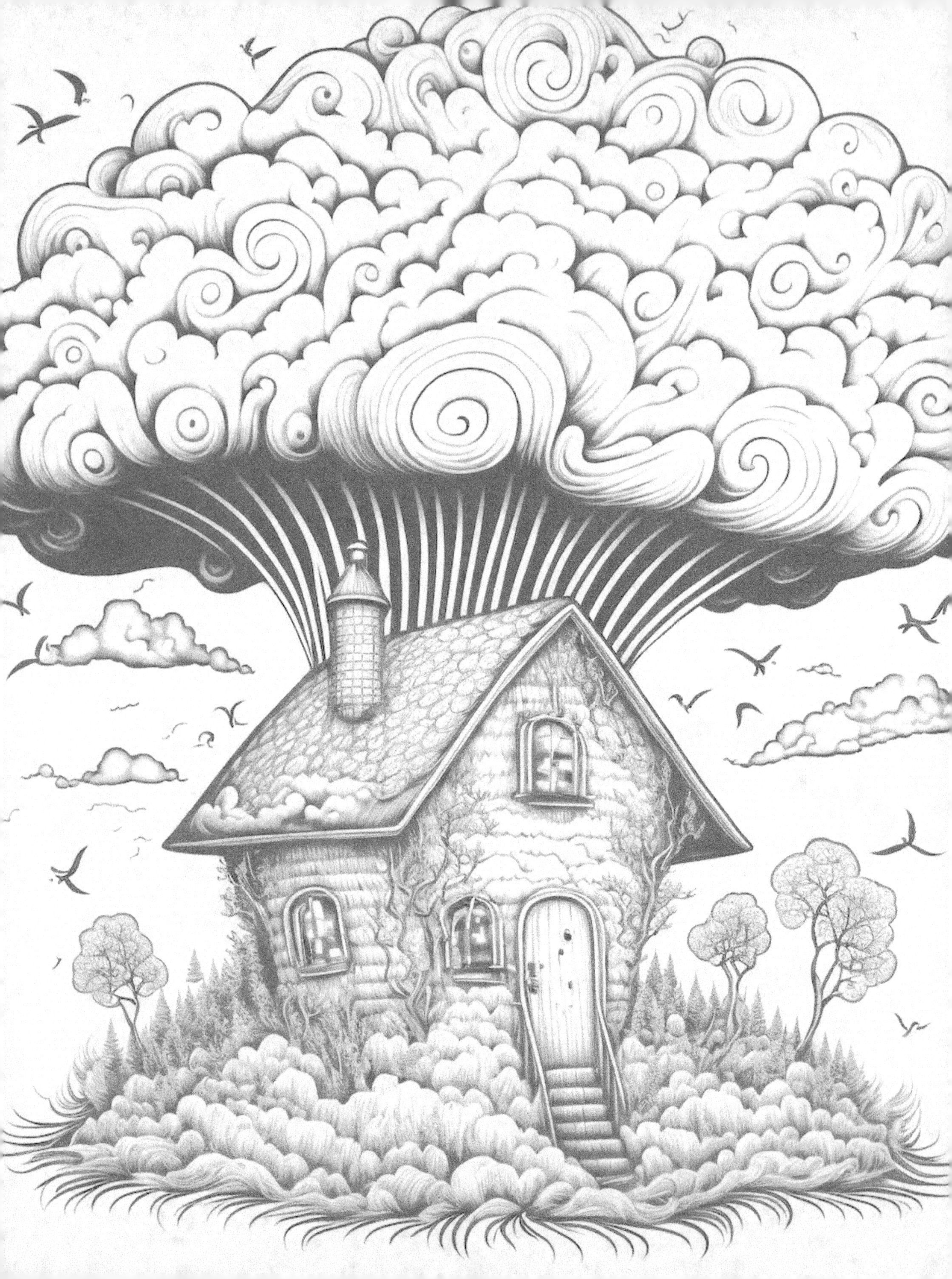

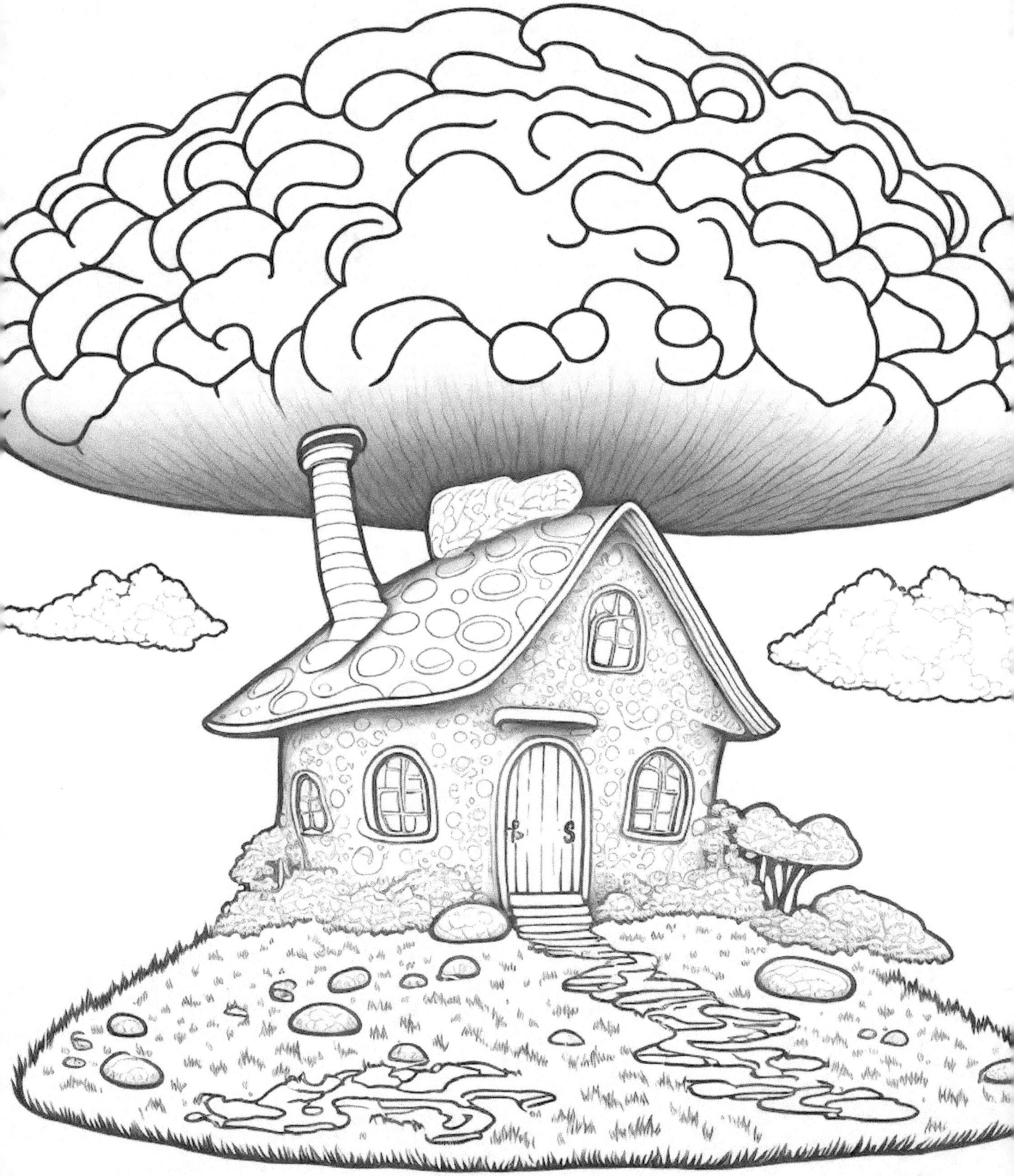

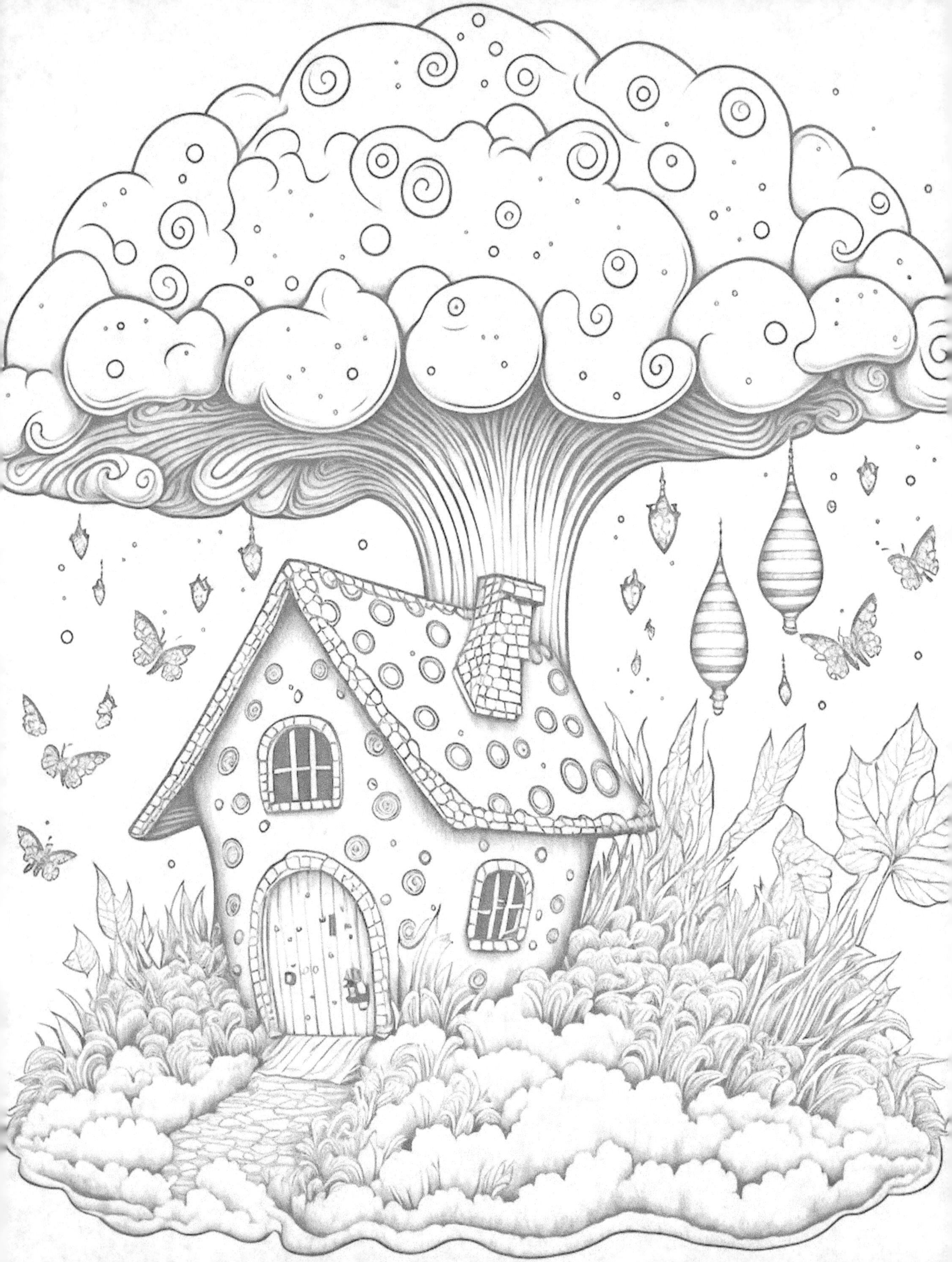

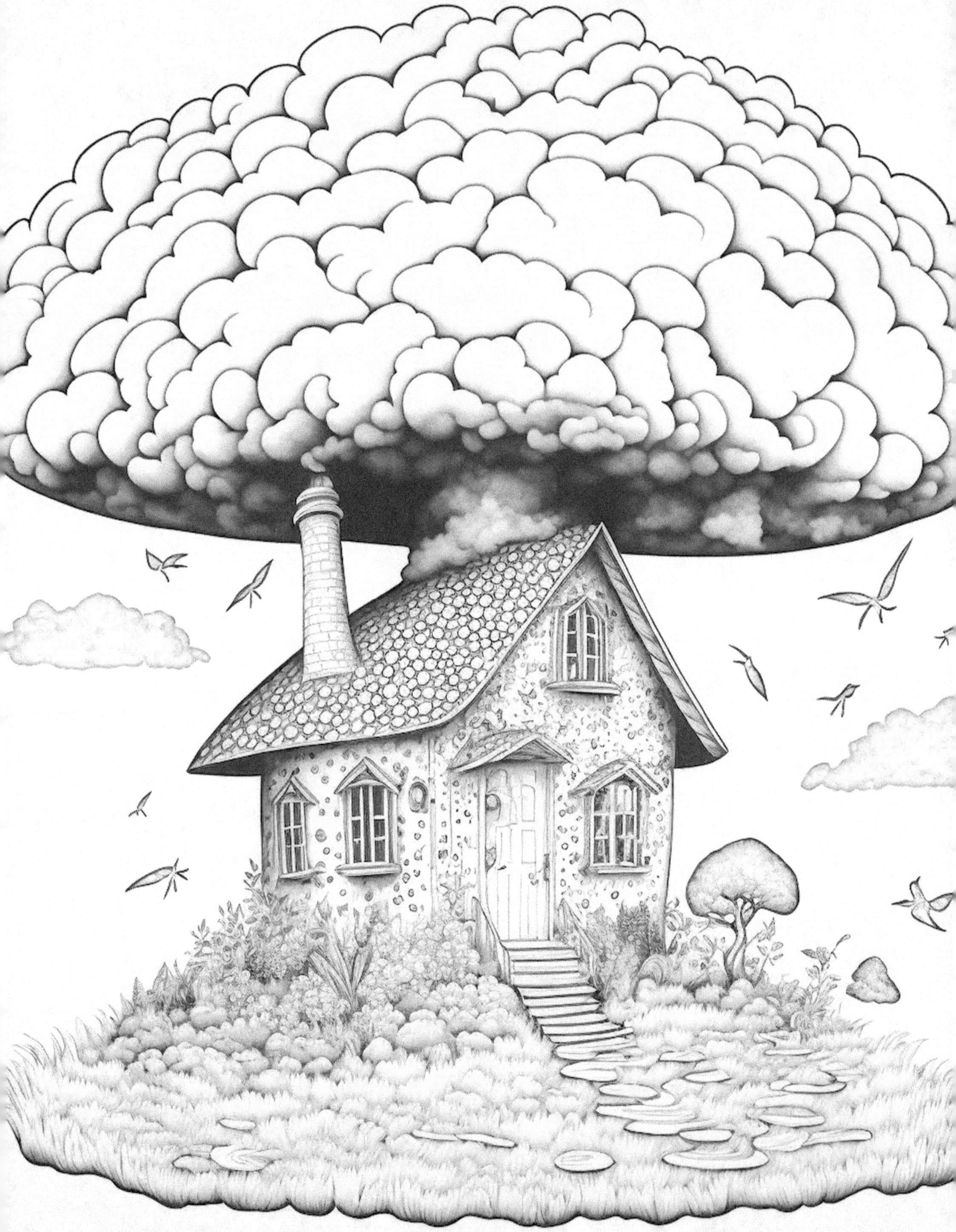

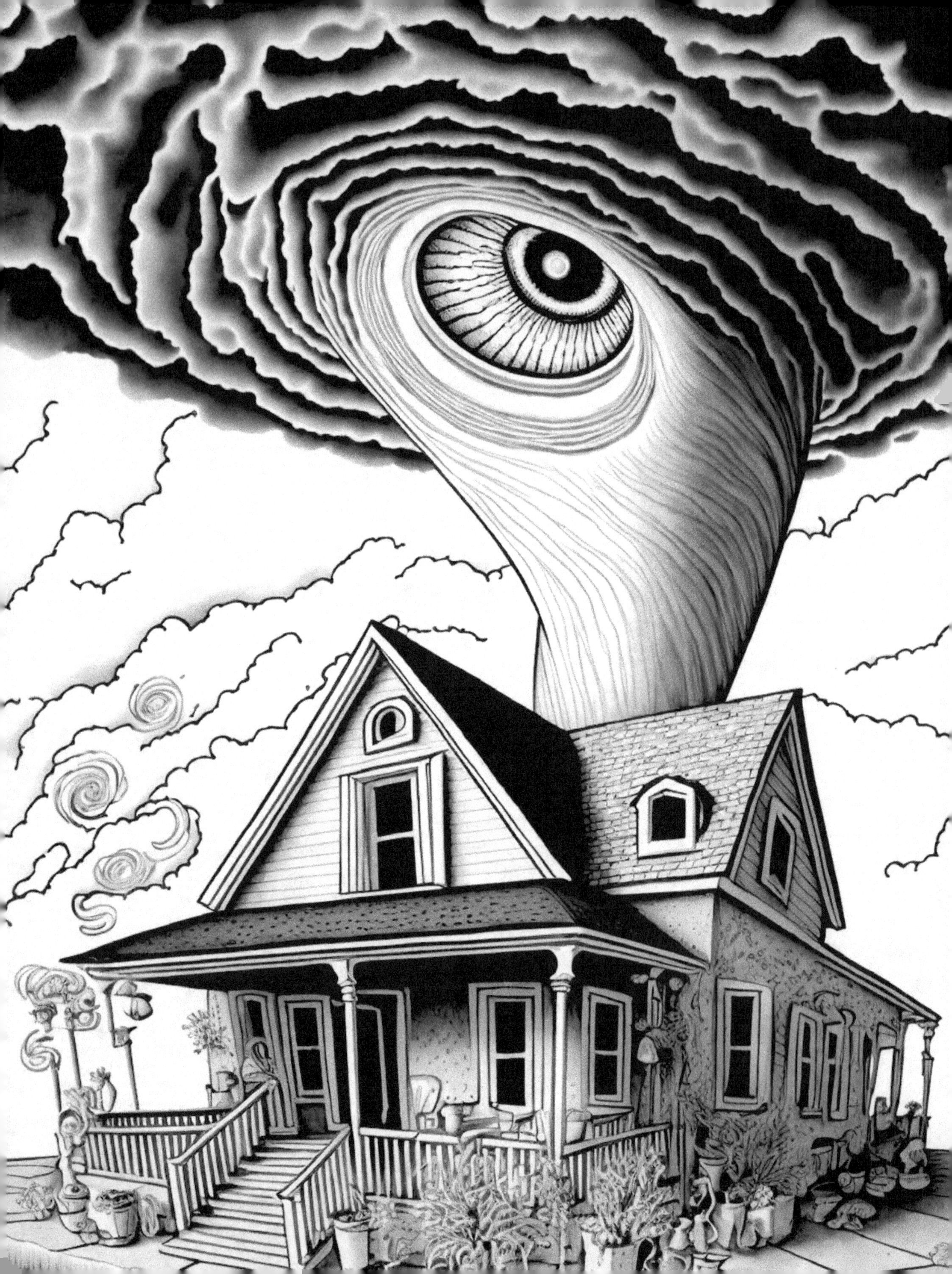

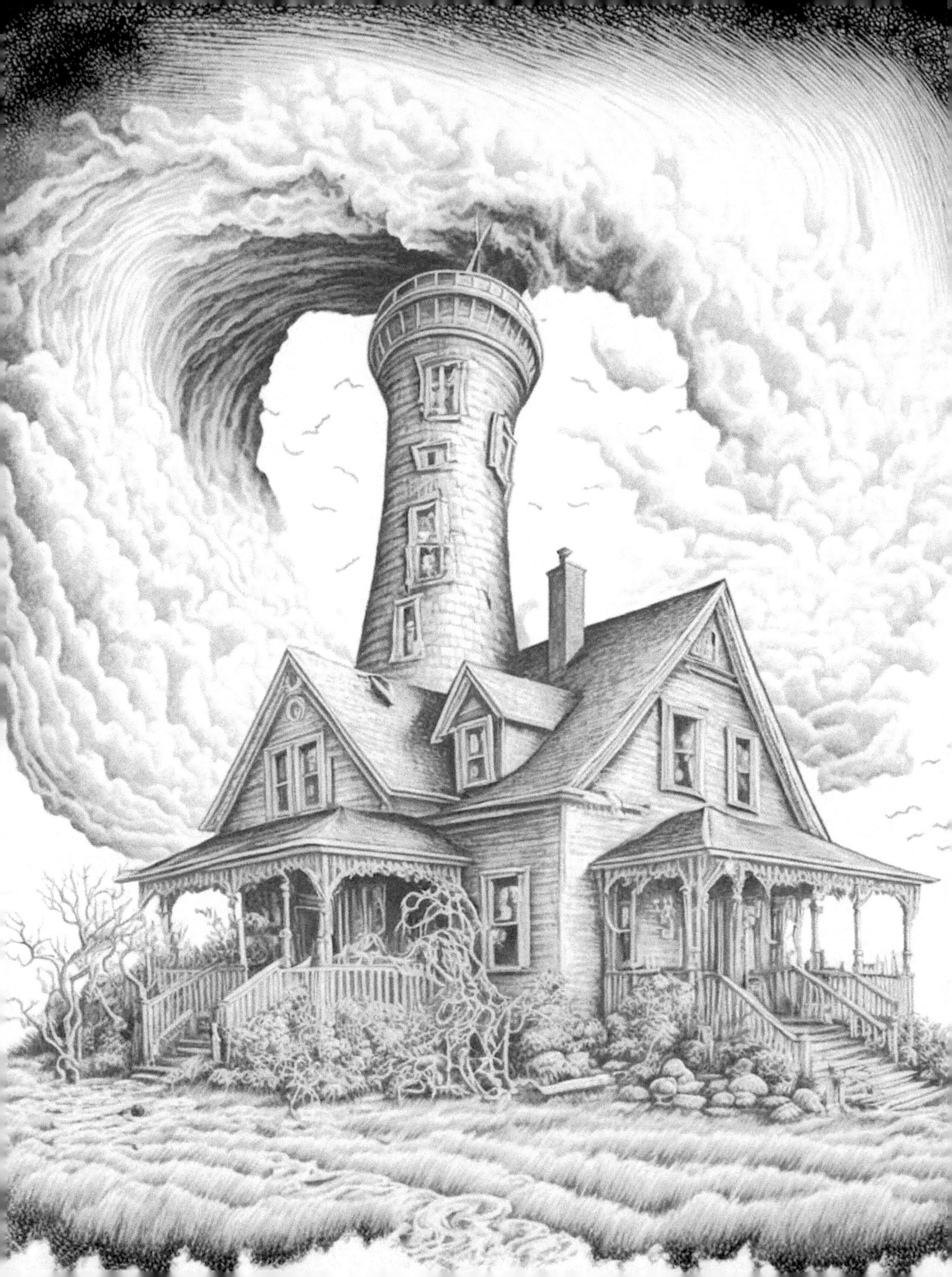

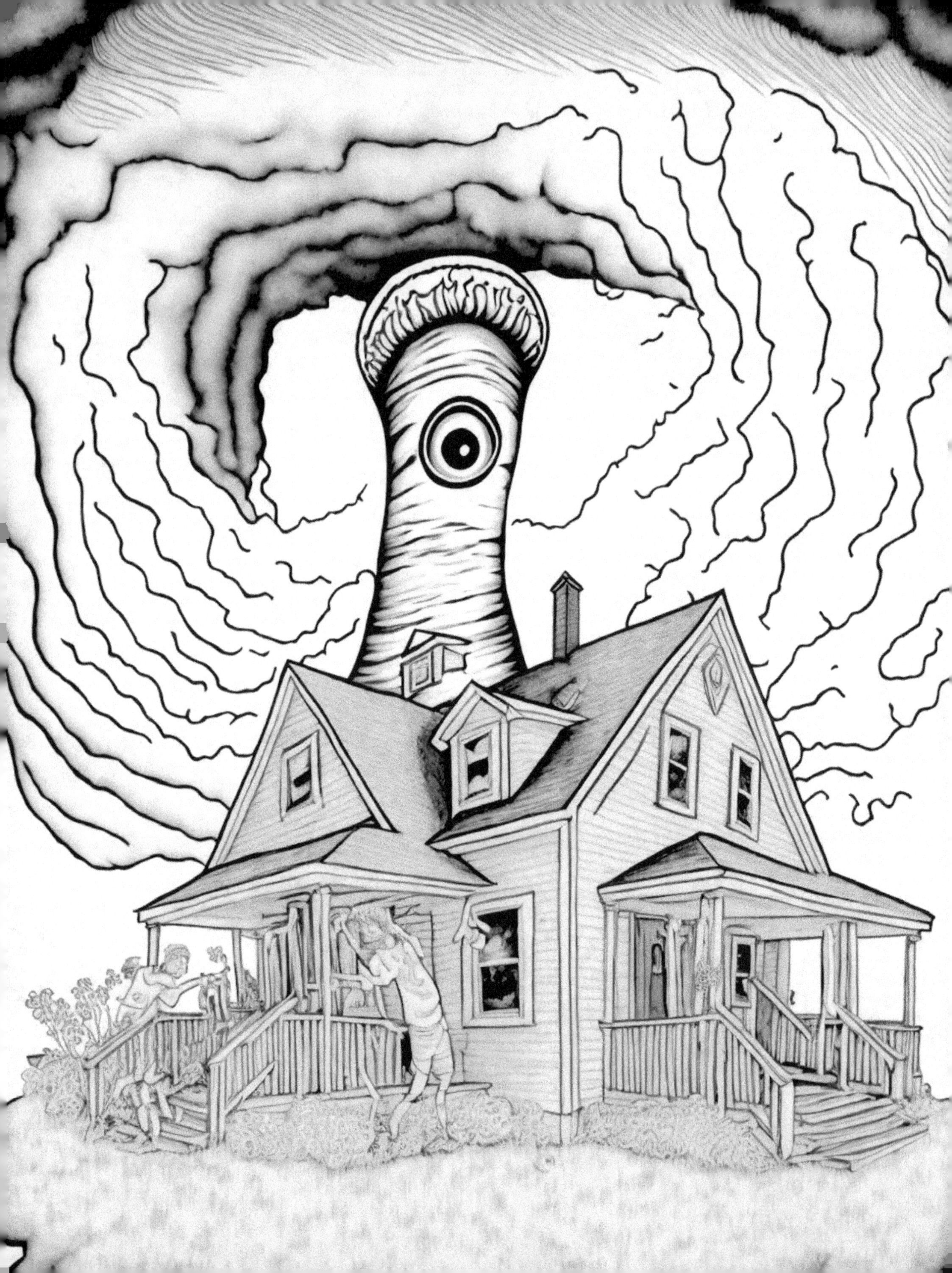

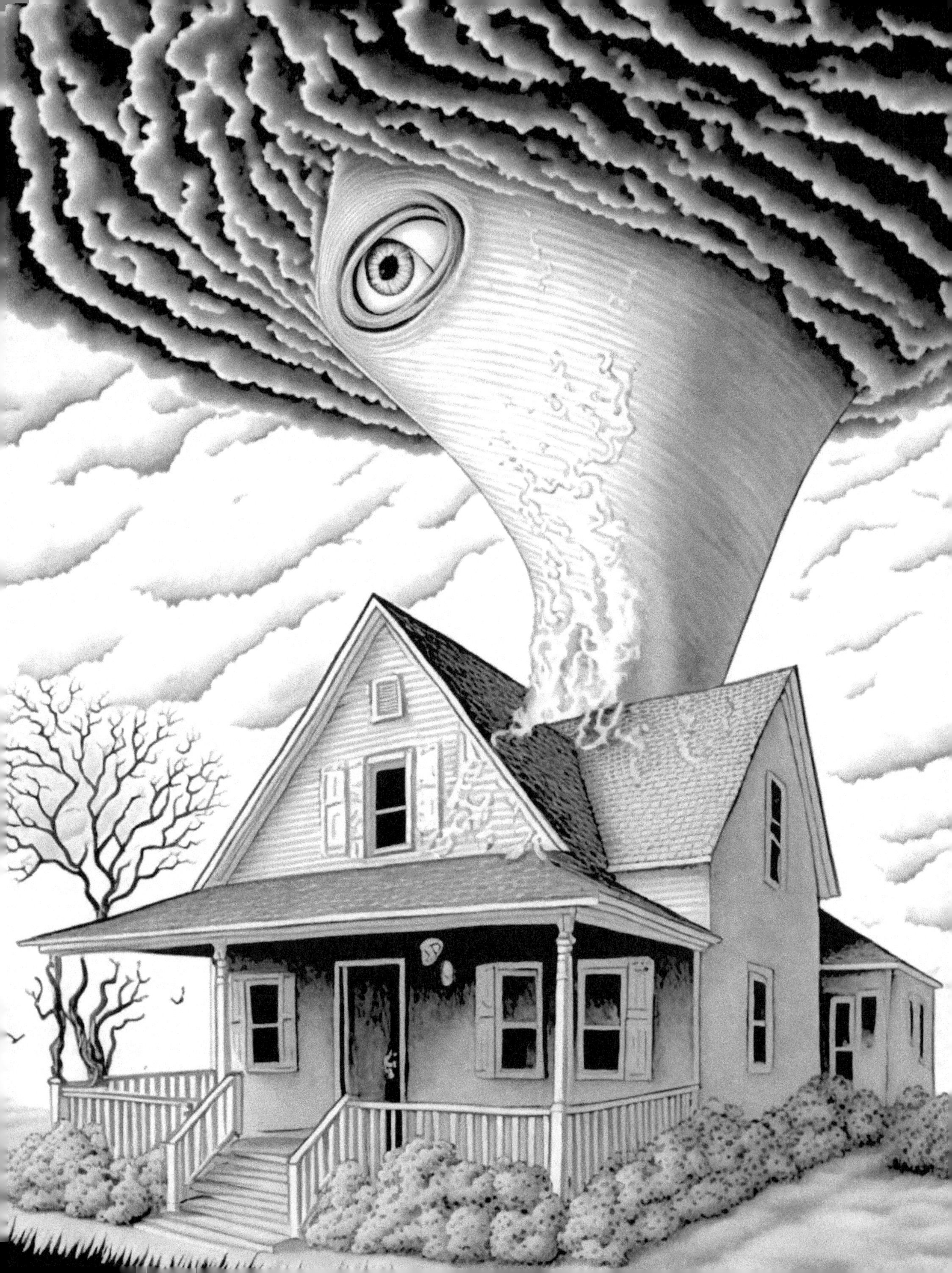

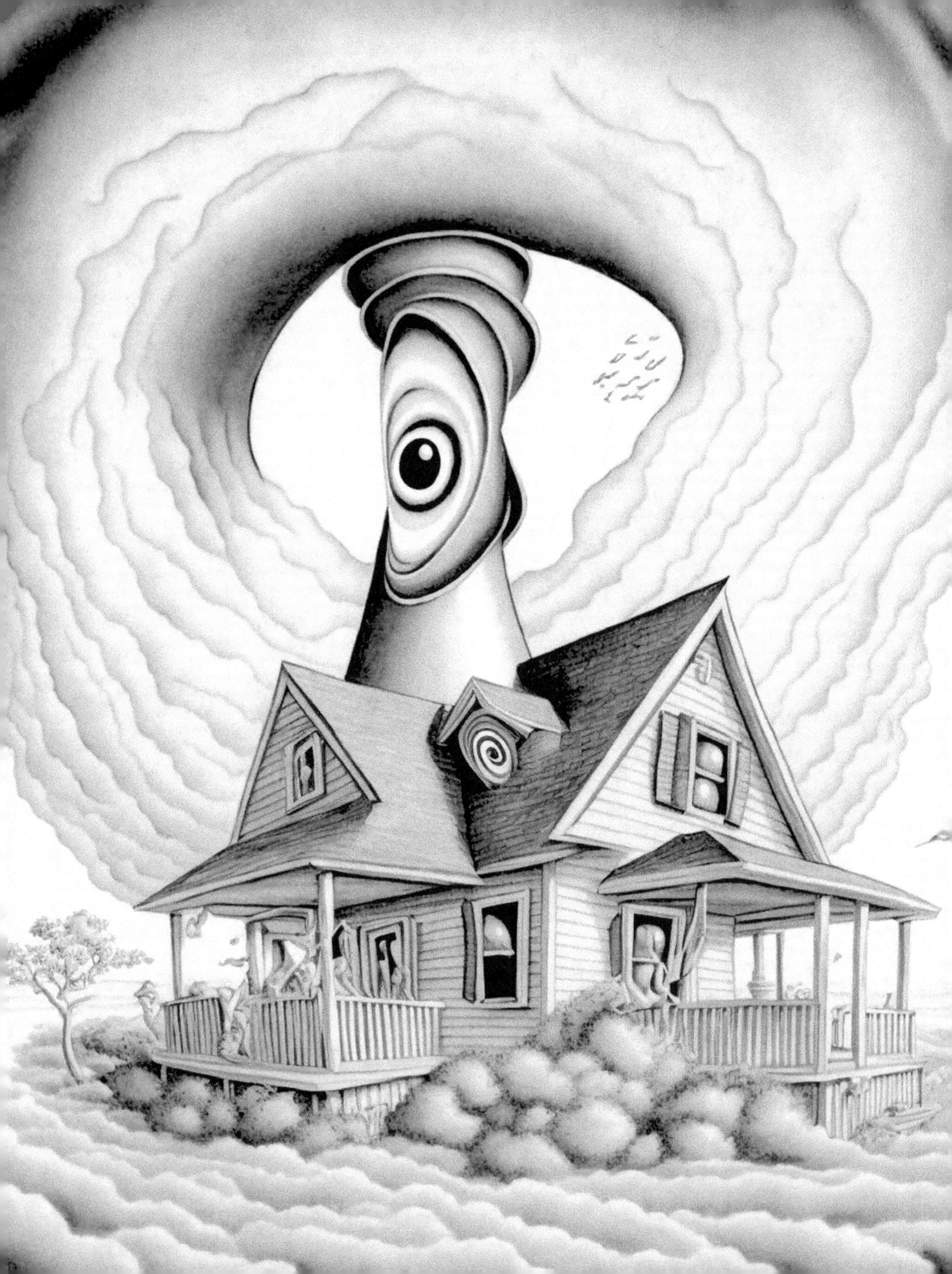

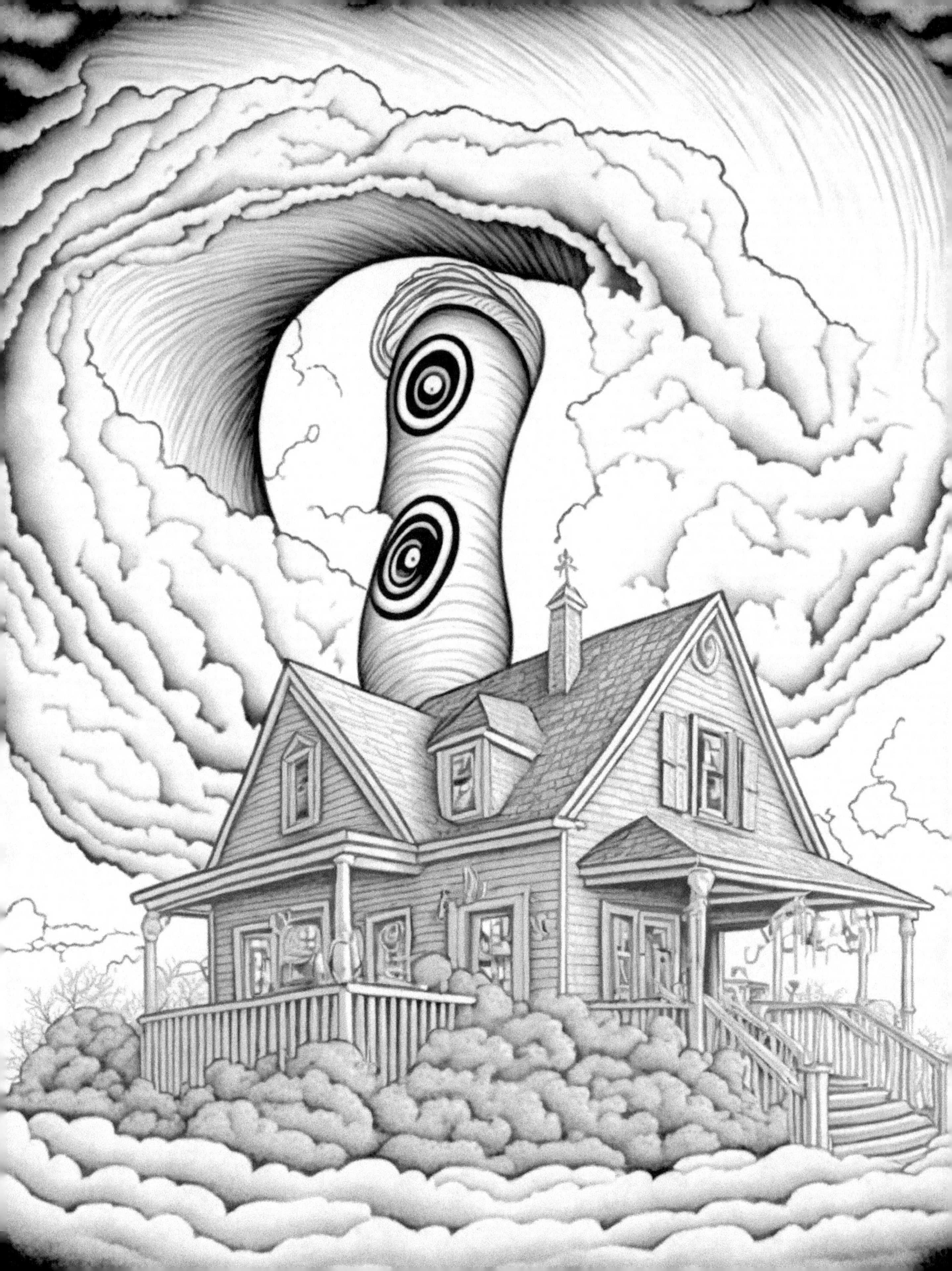

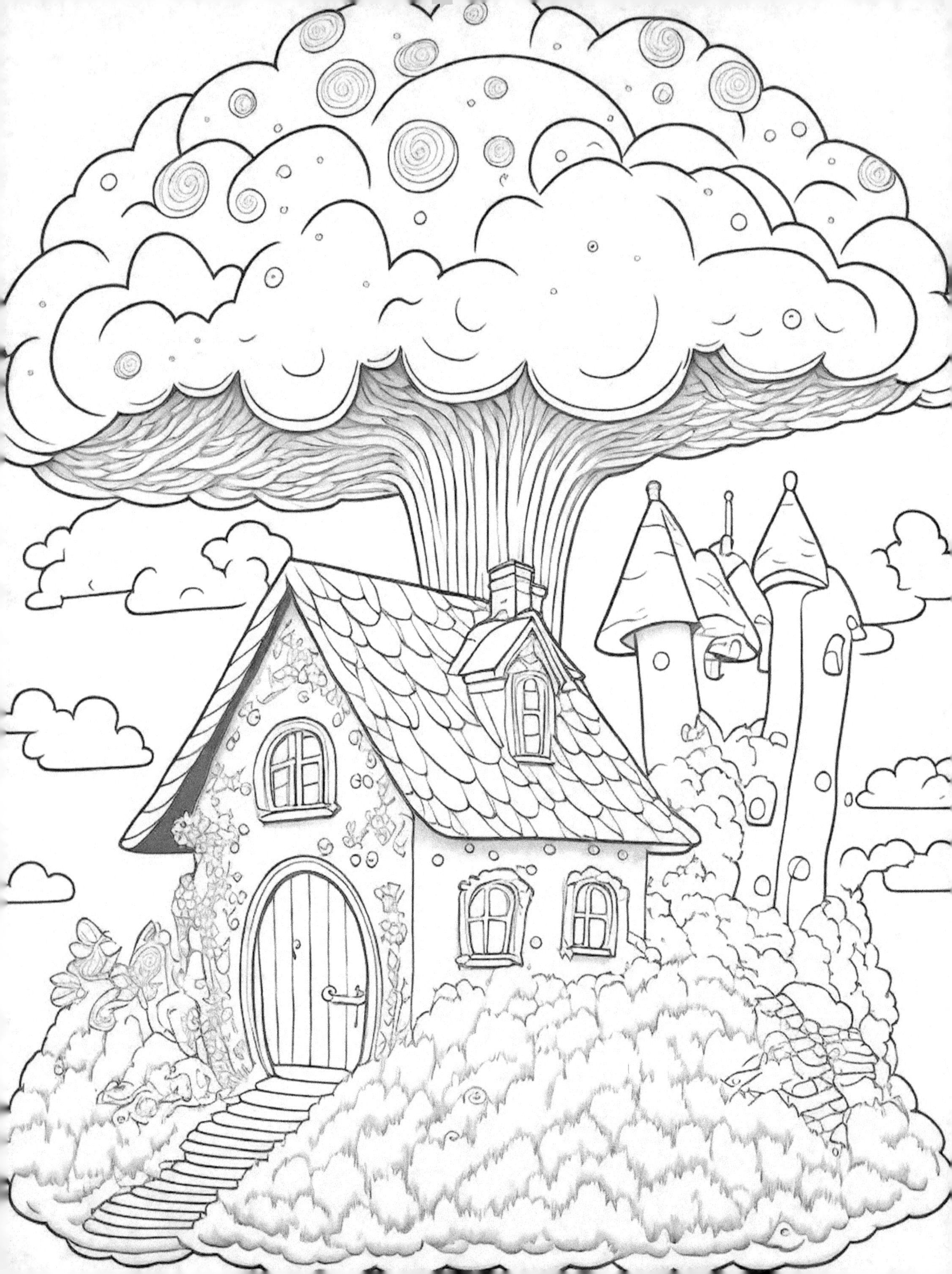

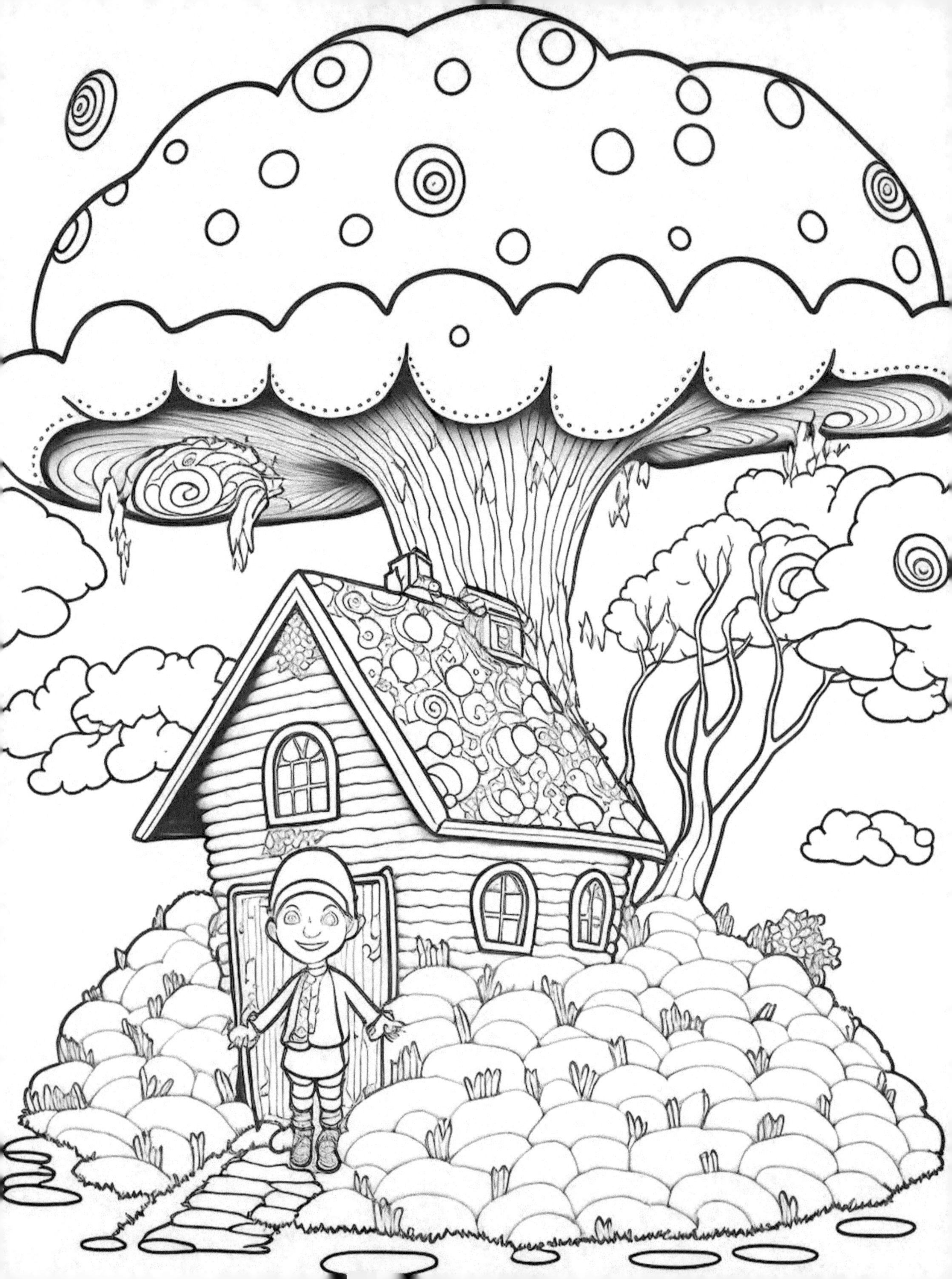

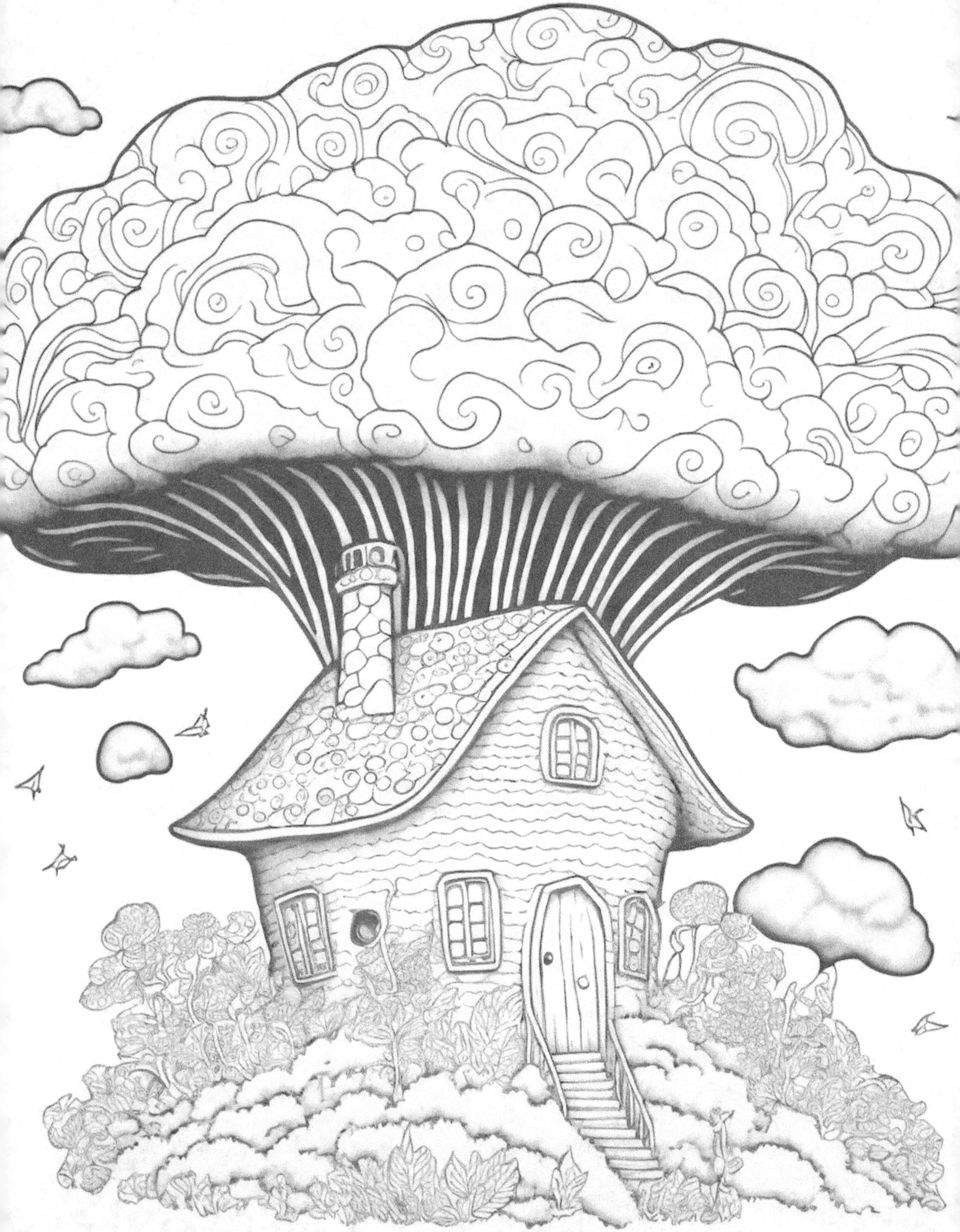

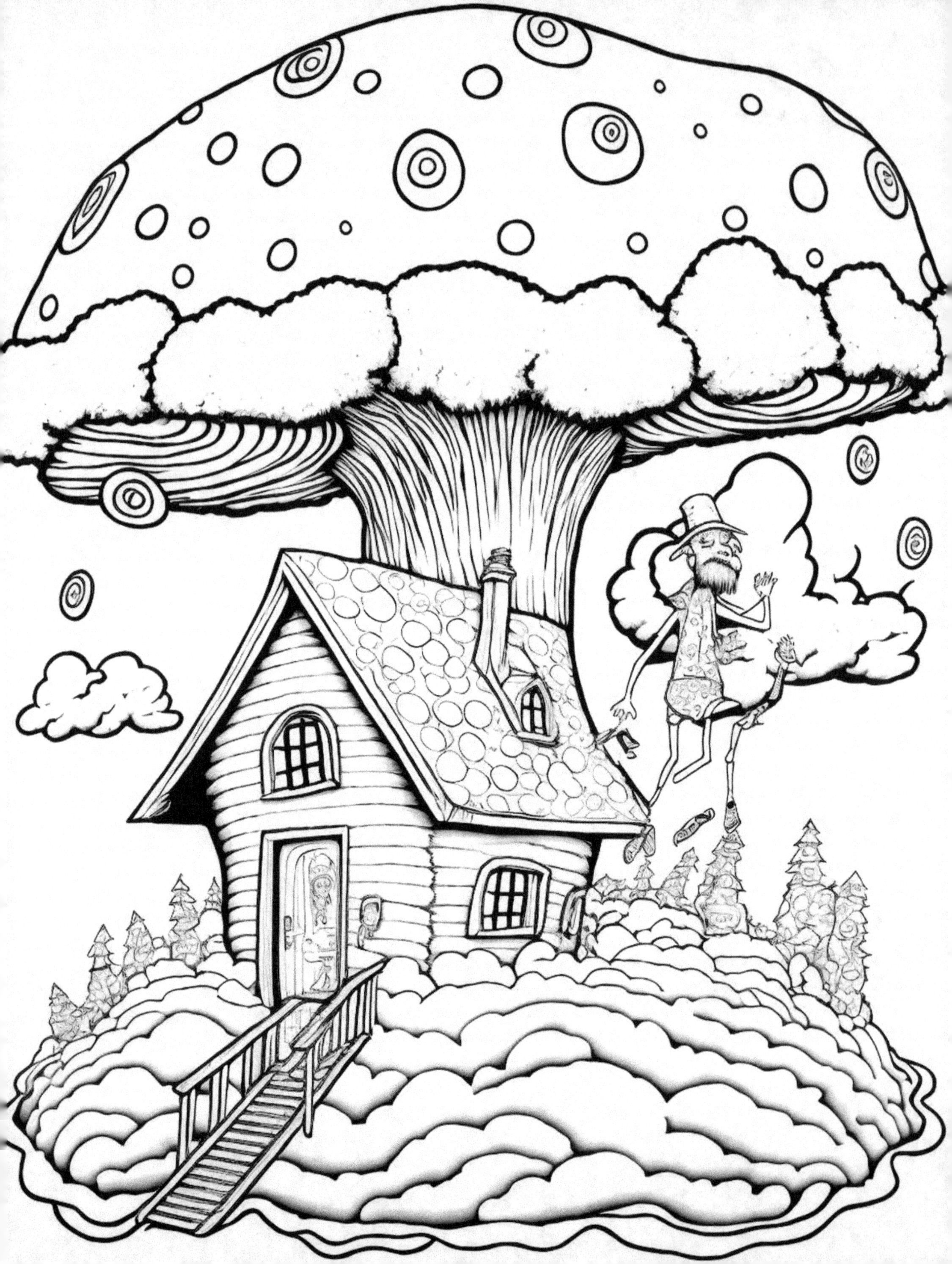

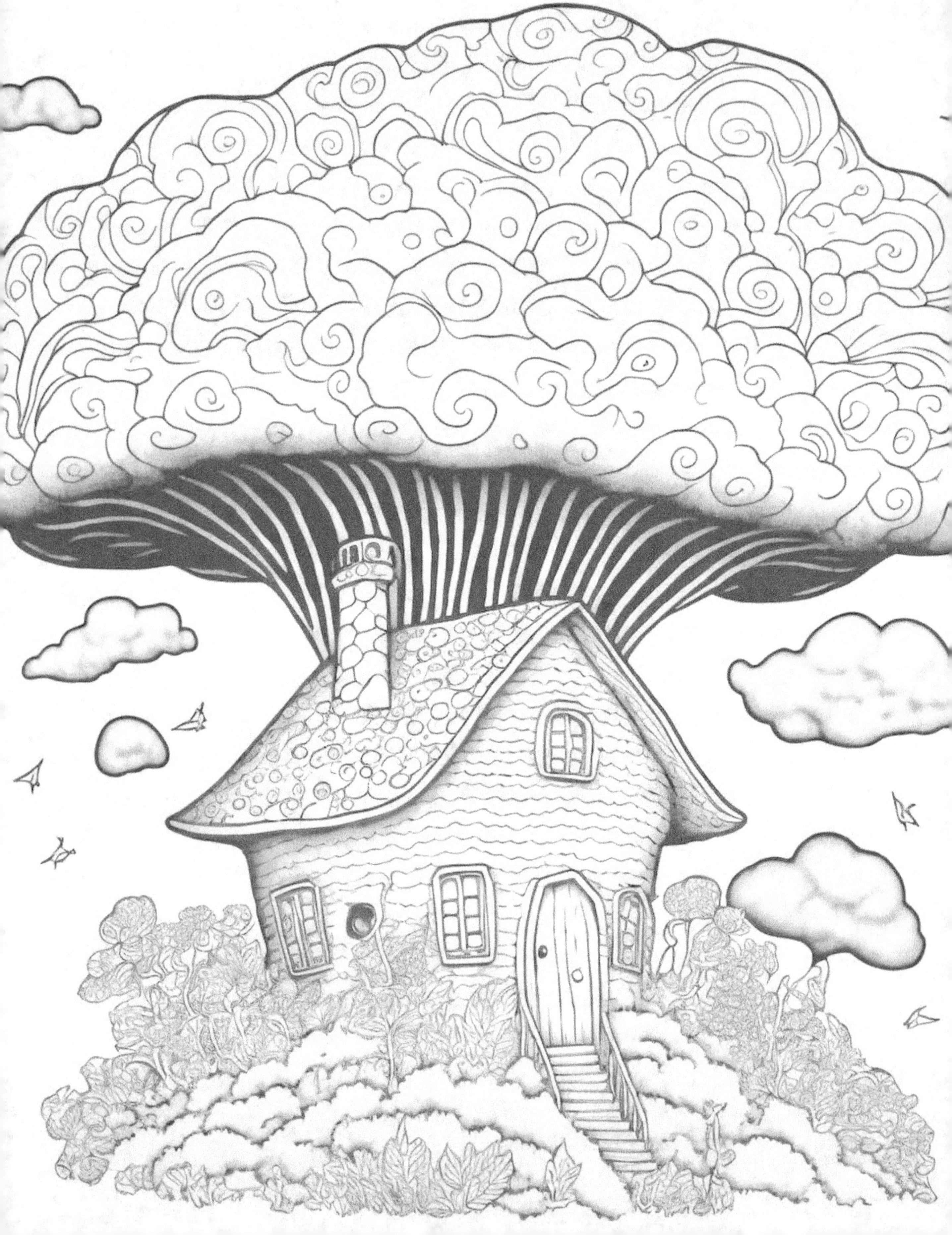

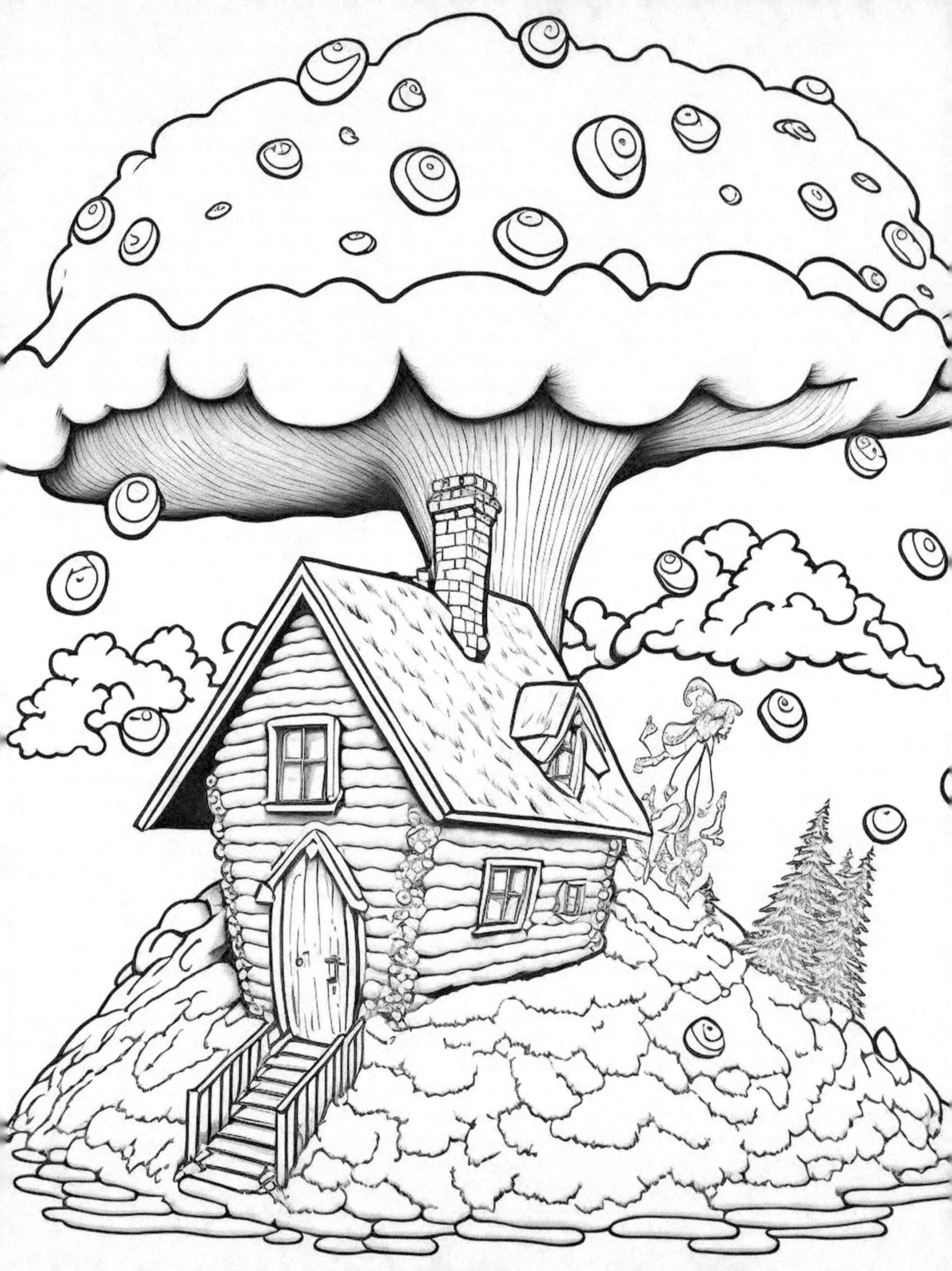

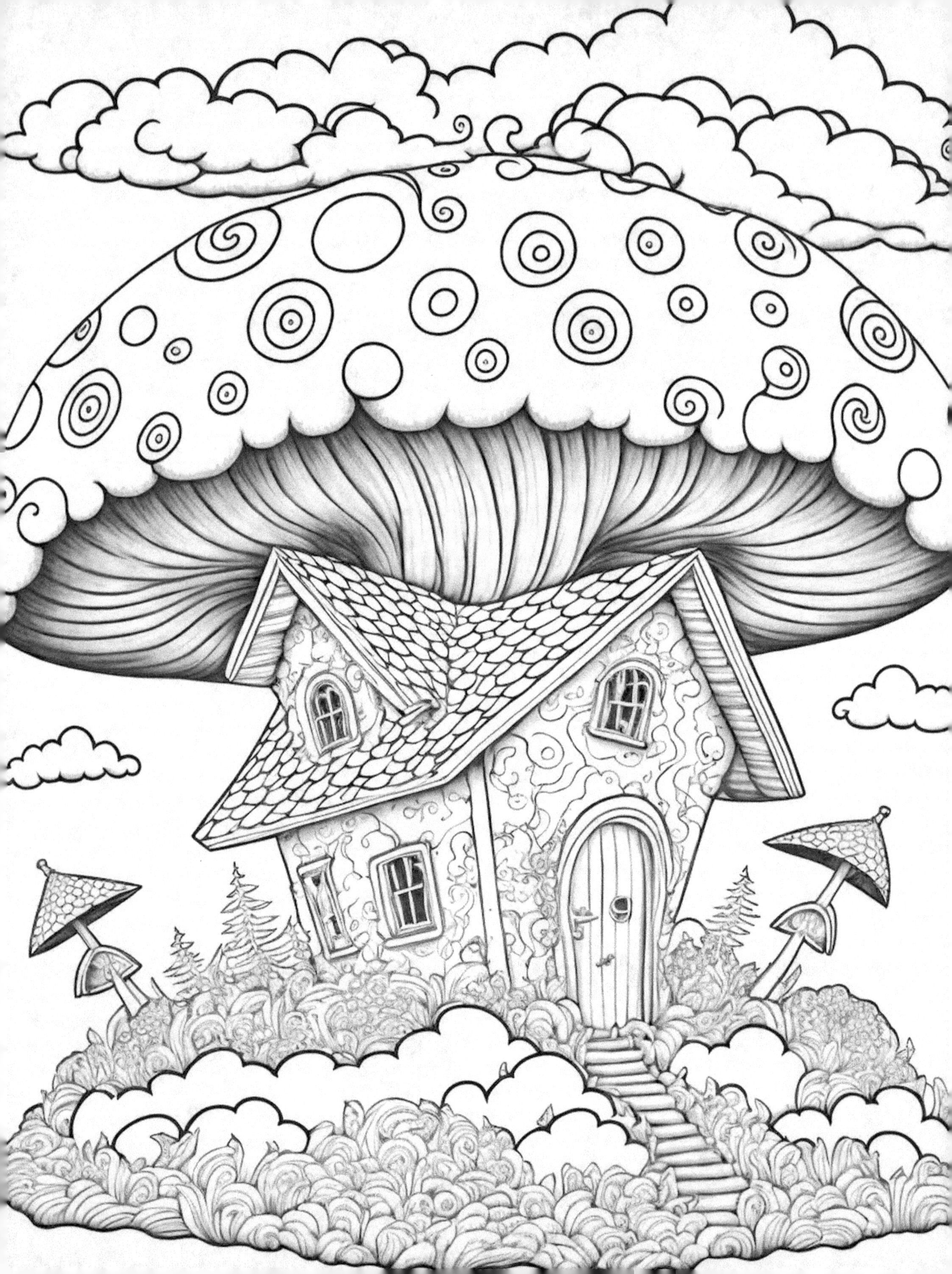

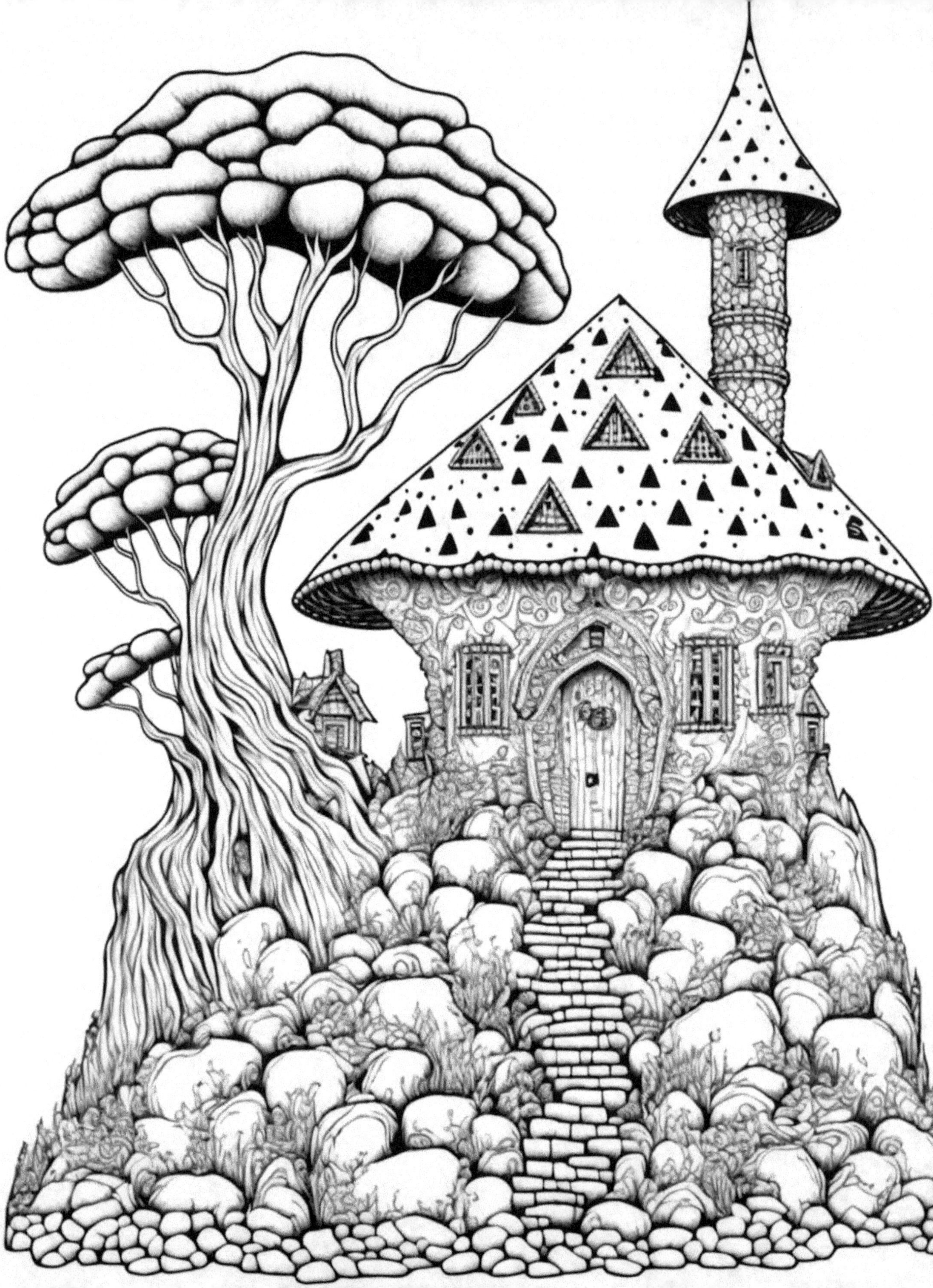

www.ingramcontent.com/pod-product-compliance
Lightning Source LLC
Chambersburg PA
CBHW080517220526
45465CB00006B/2517
9798374549447